Stained Glass at York Minster

Stained Glass at York Minster

Sarah Brown

SCALA

IN ASSOCIATION WITH THE DEAN AND CHAPTER OF YORK

First published in 1999
by Scala Publishers Ltd
143–149 Great Portland Street
London WIN 5FB

Distributed in the USA and Canada by
Antique Collectors' Club
Market Street Industrial Park
Wappingers Falls
NY 12590, USA

ISBN 1 85759 220 4

Edited by Antony Wood
Designed by Sara Robin
Printed and bound in Italy
by Sfera International Srl

Frontispiece: window in the nave (n27),
depicting the activities of the Penancers

AUTHOR'S ACKNOWLEDGEMENTS

I would like to thank in particular my colleague Dr Tom French,
formerly of the Royal Commission on the Historical Monuments of
England, for his helpful comments on this text and for discussions
on the Minster and its windows over many years. Canon John Toy
also made a number of helpful observations. Any errors in the text
are, of course, my own. My RCHME colleague Bob Skingle
undertook much of the photography for this book, greatly facilitated
by Mrs Ann Willey, Dr Peter Newman and Penny Winton and the
staff of the York Glaziers' Trust. Artwork has been provided by
Amanda Daws. Mrs Louise Hampson of the York Minster Archive
has provided advice and assistance concerning the Dean and
Chapter's photographic collections.

Sarah Brown
January 1999

Contents

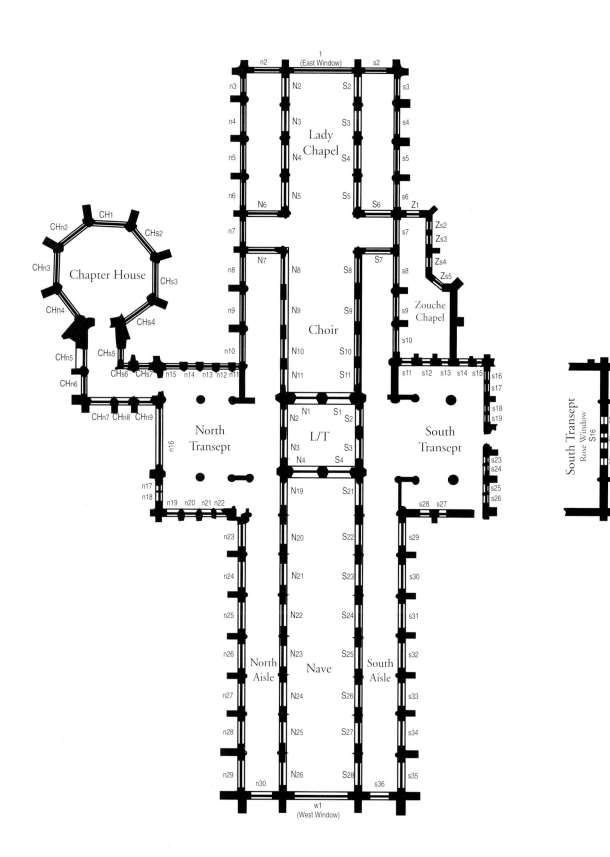

PLAN OF THE WINDOWS OF YORK MINSTER

(Corpus Vitrearum Medii Aevi numbering system)

The numbers in this plan are referred to in the text

Preface

The city of York boasts one of Europe's greatest concentrations of medieval stained glass and the Minster houses the single largest collection, representing the best in stained glass design and craftsmanship from the late twelfth century to the very eve of the Reformation. With well over 100 windows containing stained glass, it is York Minster that, more than almost any other great church in Britain, can offer a glimpse of the medieval vision of the church on earth as a foretaste of the heavenly Jerusalem, a translucent structure 'like unto clear glass' (Revelation 21: 18). The Minster's windows continued to be admired long after the cultural and religious milieu in which they were conceived had undergone drastic change. In 1697 the well-travelled Celia Fiennes declared that the Minster was possessed of 'the greatest curiosity for Windows I ever saw', a view shared by many generations of visitors to the Minster in the intervening centuries.

The building of the medieval Minster and the glazing of its windows were a collaborative enterprise which brought together churchmen, kings and nobles, laymen and women and the craftsmen and citizens of York. The care of the windows in the late twentieth century continues to be a collaboration, in which craftsmen and women, theologians and scholars all play their part. In the Middle Ages the windows served to greet, instruct and inspire the medieval pilgrim. This book will add to the enjoyment and appreciation of the many thousands of modern pilgrims who follow in their footsteps.

THE DEAN OF YORK
The Very Reverend Raymond Furnell

From Edwin's Conversion to the Twelfth Century

The pre-Conquest Minster

When Wilfrid was made Bishop of York in 670 he found the stone church begun by the first Christian King of Northumbria, Edwin, c.627 and later completed by King Oswald, in a ruinous state; 'the ridge of the roof, owing to its age let the water through, the windows were unglazed and the birds flew in and out, building their nests' says Wilfrid's biographer, Eddi. Wilfrid set about restoring the church, replacing pierced slabs and linen cloths with glass. It is unlikely that the glaziers were local craftsmen, for when in 674 Abbot Benedict Biscop founded the monastery of Monkwearmouth, he sent to Gaul for craftsmen to glaze his new church, having been unable to find anyone skilled in the craft in Britain. Both Benedict Biscop and Bishop Wilfrid were adherents of the Roman tradition. Both men had visited Rome itself and regarded glass windows as fitting amenities for a major church.

Literary sources offer little information as to the nature of the Saxon Minster's windows. Eddi records only that they prevented the birds from entering the church while allowing the light to shine within. Glass fragments excavated at Anglo-Saxon sites at Monkwearmouth, Jarrow and Escomb in Northumberland are coloured but unpainted and it is likely that the windows of Wilfrid's church, as yet undiscovered by archaeology, were also glazed in this way.

The church of Thomas of Bayeux

By the time Archbishop Thomas was consecrated in 1070, the Saxon cathedral had once again been reduced to a dilapidated state, as a result of Danish incursion, fire and unrest in the north following the Conquest, and only three of its canons remained alive. Thomas, formerly treasurer of Bayeux Cathedral, re-roofed and restored the Saxon church, but in 1075 it was so badly damaged by fire that in c.1080 Thomas began to rebuild on an entirely new site. It is this church, completed c.1100, that lies beneath the present Minster and was excavated between 1966 and 1973.

Reconstructions of Thomas's church (2) show it to have had large numbers of small, deep-set, single lancet openings in its three storeys. No literary sources shed light on the nature of the cathedral's glazing and almost nothing of its superstructure survives. That it was glazed with coloured, painted glass can be surmised from the discovery of five fragments of blue glass in the area to the north of the eleventh-century north transept north wall. These pieces bear traces of what might be painted drapery or foliage. Very little stained glass survives from the late eleventh and early twelfth centuries, but the four monumental figures of prophets of about 1100 that survive in Augsburg Cathedral perhaps suggest what Thomas's stained glass might have looked like.

The Twelfth-Century Minster

In 1154 Roger of Pont L'Evêque (1154–81), Archdeacon of Canterbury, became Archbishop of York. Roger sought to enhance the prestige of the northern province

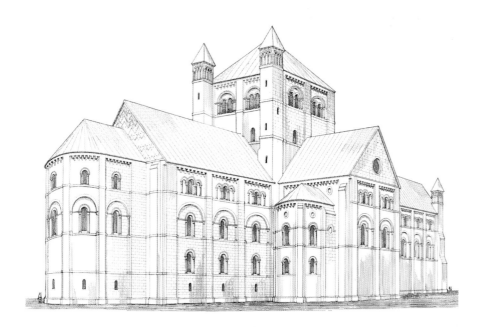

and its cathedral at the expense of Canterbury, which claimed ecclesiastical supremacy, and Scotland, which claimed ecclesiastical independence of the northern province. This prestige was to be given architectural expression and, early in his archiepiscopacy, Roger began to rebuild his cathedral church, constructing a new eastern arm of seven bays with crypt, and adding western towers to the nave. In scale the new choir emulated that of Canterbury, while in style it was one of the most innovative buildings of its day, combining elements derived from the early Gothic churches of northern France and the great monastic churches of the Cistercians in the north of England, with their familiarity with the Burgundian houses of the Order. The earliest parts of Ripon Minster, another of Roger's architectural projects, give some impression of what the twelfth-century choir of York must have looked like. The western parts of Roger's crypt survive beneath the present Minster and, with their complex and richly decorated piers, hint at the splendour of his church.

Over fifty panels of late twelfth-century stained glass survive, reused by later Minster builders. The largest number are located in the clerestory of the fourteenth-century nave, where they have been since at least the 1690s, when they were recorded by the seventeenth-century antiquary James Torr, in a manuscript now in the library of York Minster. Like a number of pieces of Romanesque sculpture, the panels were reused at high levels in the new nave, where their archaic style would have been less noticeable. They have been cut down to fit their new locations, but were originally circular, quatrefoil and vesica-shaped, accompanied by wide foliage borders, of which about fifteen sections survive.

The remains of about eight picture cycles have so far been identified. There are four scenes of events following the Crucifixion (the three Marys at the tomb, the supper at Emmaus, a group of disciples(?) and the miraculous draught of fishes (5), and a number of episodes from the life and miracles of Saints Benedict, Nicholas of Myra (4), Martin of Tours and possibly Richarius of St Riquier (near Amiens). A seated king, all that remains of a Tree of Jesse, is now displayed in the foundations (1).

ABOVE
4 A scene from the
miracles of St Nicholas
of Myra, *c*.1180 (S27)

OPPOSITE
5 The miraculous draught
of fishes, *c*.1180 (S26)

A single Old Testament scene, Daniel in the lion's den miraculously fed by the prophet Habakkuk, is located in the Five Sisters window in the north transept (10), to which it was probably moved in the seventeenth century. Finally, twelve scenes depict the Last Judgement, including trumpeting angels, St Peter and St Paul, the jaws of Hell and groups of the dammed led off to torment by demons.

That these panels should be associated with the work of Roger's archiepiscopacy is borne out by comparison with other work of the last quarter of the twelfth century. Such comparisons demonstrate both the international and the regional character of York glass-painting at this date. In its symmetry and the disposition of foliage, for example, the York Jesse Tree panel (1) closely resembles the famous Jesse Tree in Abbot Suger's abbey of Saint-Denis (c.1145) and the similar Tree in the west façade of Chartres Cathedral (c.1145–55). The York panel is thus the earliest surviving example of this subject in English stained glass. The late Dr Peter Newton has shown that the three scenes from the life of St Benedict are indebted to an eleventh-century life of the saint made for the Benedictine Abbey of Monte Cassino (Vatican Library, Cod. Lat. 1202). A scene very similar to the York panel depicting St Benedict in a cave fed by Romanus was also depicted in glass at Saint-Denis (a panel now in Raby Castle chapel). Decorative motifs used in the York panels also suggest a familiarity with Continental art and in particular with glass-painting in northern France.

RIGHT
6 A scene from the St Benedict window, c.1180 (S25)

FAR RIGHT
7 Two trumpeting angels from the Last Judgement(?), c.1180 (S23)

LEFT
8 Exuberant border
designs of c.1180

BELOW
9 St John the Evangelist
from the Chapter House
of St Mary's Abbey,
York, c.1180–5. (York,
The Yorkshire Museum)

Comparable border designs survive in the Moses window at Saint-Denis, in the clerestory of St Rémi at Reims and at Le Mans Cathedral.

In acknowledging the links between York and the Continent at this date, it would be a mistake to overlook the importance of a specifically northern English context for these exceptional panels. It is clear that the decorative and figural arts flourished in late twelfth-century York and Durham. Archbishop Roger's contemporary, Bishop Hugh du Puiset of Durham (1153–95), a former treasurer of York Minster, glazed the apse windows of his cathedral with very similar glass, now lost. The stone figures from the twelfth-century west front of York Minster (heavily weathered and many now replaced by nineteenth-century copies), the reused twelfth-century Evangelist symbols (two placed internally above the west window and two externally on the south-west tower), together with the closely related figures from the Chapter House of St Mary's Abbey (9) and twenty-four sculptures at Guisborough Priory, provide ample evidence that York was a centre of sculptural excellence in the period c.1170–90. These monumental figures with their looping U-shaped drapery folds have long been compared to the stained glass. No paintings of comparable scale have survived in York, but useful comparisons with two-dimensional works can be found in a group of manuscripts which, on the evidence of their calendars, were made in the north of England and perhaps in the diocese of York. The figures in the manuscripts (in the Bodleian Library, Oxford, the Royal Library, Copenhagen and Durham Cathedral Library) share the heavily modelled faces with long noses, deep-set eyes, angular brows and deeply furrowed expressions with an inclination to side-long glances that also characterize the Minster glass.

Despite their Continental affinities, the York border designs are distinctive for their use of modelling washes on the exterior surfaces of the glass and for the higher proportion of white glass used. Comparison with the architectural decoration of Roger's choir provides a useful parallel for the use of strongly interlacing lozenges as a framework for the foliage decoration. A broadly similar structure is found in

10 Daniel in the lion's den, miraculously fed by the Prophet Habakkuk, c.1180 (now in n16)

the decoration of the somewhat earlier elaborate north jamb of a doorway at the west end of the northern ambulatory of the Romanesque crypt of York Minster (3) and on the chapter house door of St Mary's Abbey.

The loss of their original architectural context hampers establishment of an accurate chronology for these panels, and it cannot be discounted that work continued for some years after Roger's death in 1181. However, the interregnum and troubled tenure of his successor Geoffrey Plantagenet (1191–1212) were periods less conducive to artistic patronage. The loss of Roger's building also makes it difficult to reconstruct the original disposition of these twelfth-century panels, although comparison with *in situ* schemes of similar date offers some clues. One location for the Tree of Jesse might have been on the north side of the flat east wall of Roger's choir. With flanking figures of prophets and foliage borders, this window could have been as much as two metres wide. The central east window might have accommodated the scenes of Christ's Passion and Resurrection. The single Old Testament scene suggests that typological arrangements were favoured as the Daniel scene (10) is a type of the Annunciation, although there is no trace of an Infancy cycle among the surviving panels. The lives of the saints may have been arranged in the choir windows or in the crypt, where many altars were situated.

This hypothesis is not without its problems, however. The eastern bay of Roger's choir was not demolished until c.1364 and its western bays were in use until the 1390s, by which time the new nave had been completed and glazed. If the Romanesque panels were glazed into the nave clerestory in the early fourteenth century, an alternative original location for them may have to be considered. Excavation has shown that the eleventh-century transepts were altered in the twelfth century, perhaps resulting in reglazing. Thomas's aisleless nave may also have been reglazed to make it look more up to date. The subsequent demolition of both of these structures would have released stained glass for reuse in the fourteenth-century nave.

The original arrangement of Last Judgement panels presents particular difficulties, as it is a comparatively rare subject in narrative lancets at this date. While an oculus is one possibility, the two panels containing groups of apostles require a central figure of Christ, only possible in a horizontal arrangement, three panels wide. Three panels, with borders, would have required a window of considerable size, and a window in Roger's west work, between the western towers, at the opposite end of the cathedral to the redemptive Passion scenes at the east end, is a possibility.

11 Six types of geometric unpainted grisaille, probably late twelfth century, reused, with additions, in the early fourteenth-century nave clerestory. Drawing by J. A. Knowles

Before we leave the twelfth-century glass, brief mention should be made of a collection of unpainted geometric grisaille panels (11), inserted with the figurative glass into the fourteenth-century nave clerestory. This kind of glazing enjoyed a long period of popularity, and at Salisbury Cathedral, for example, continued in use into the second quarter of the thirteenth century. Indeed, three of the York patterns are closely related to designs at Salisbury. This type of glazing was probably once quite common wherever cheaper, simpler and lighter windows were required, although it was also commonly associated with the Cistercian Order, which, from the middle of the twelfth century, discouraged the use of coloured and painted window glass in its churches.

Close parallels to the York panels are to be found among surviving Cistercian glazing and tile patterns. Two York designs are almost identical to patterns in windows in the French Cistercian churches at Obazine, La Bénissons-Dieu and Pontigny. The design of interlocking circles at York is also found in a late twelfth-century Benedictine context at Orbais and on a relief tile from the Cistercian nunnery at North Berwick. The collection of grisaille at York represents an important addition to our knowledge of this kind of glazing. In salvaging it, restoring it and installing it in the fourteenth-century nave, the builders of the Gothic Minster were unwittingly preserving examples of a now rare form of Medieval glazing. Even in its restored condition it provides an impression of the lost glazing of the great Cistercian churches of the north.

The Transepts

The Minster was extraordinarily lucky with its medieval archbishops, counting a number of able administrators, talented politicians and far-sighted and generous benefactors among them. After the turbulent episcopacy of Geoffrey Plantagenet and an interregnum of three years, Walter de Gray was translated from the See of Worcester in 1215, to become the longest-serving and most influential of York's thirteenth-century archbishops. Like Archbishop Roger before him, Walter de Gray (1215–55) strove to enhance the prestige of his See and stabilize and enrich his Chapter. During his tenure, a new period of building activity was initiated, involving the rebuilding of the transepts and crossing, which survive today as the earliest part of the present Minster.

It might be wondered what Archbishop de Gray and his Chapter sought to achieve in building new transepts, at the centre of the cruciform building, when it was more usual to rebuild a great church from either eastern or western extremities. The new choir was, of course, barely 40 years old when funds and building materials for the new work began to be assembled in the 1220s, and the nave, while old-fashioned, had been enhanced by the addition of new western towers, and perhaps refurbished with new stained glass. The explanation may lie in the purposes served by the new transepts and be associated with moves to secure the canonization of William Fitzherbert (d.1154), the former treasurer and Archbishop of York, buried at the east end of the nave. York had long been disadvantaged as a great cathedral church by the lack of the pilgrim attraction of a 'resident' saint. Those saintly men associated with the See and the City, such as Paulinus, Chad, Wilfrid, Oswald and John of Beverely, had all died outside York and been buried elsewhere. The thirteenth century was a period of great activity associated with saints and their shrines – Salisbury sought to have Osmund canonized, Lincoln secured the canonization of Hugh of Avalon and, most importantly of all, in 1220 Canterbury translated St Thomas Becket, canonized in 1173, to a new shrine in the newly rebuilt Trinity Chapel of the Cathedral. Archbishop de Gray was quick to act to secure a saint for York – in 1223 sweet-smelling oil was reported to have flowed from William's tomb and in 1227 Pope Honorius III declared William a saint.

The new south transept, probably under construction by 1225, provided the cathedral with a splendid new portal facing one of the busiest entrances to the Minster Close. By 1235 work had reached the Romanesque central tower, retained at its lower levels, but topped by a new belfry, and by c.1255 the north transept was probably complete. The new transepts provided a spacious assembly area for the pilgrims gathering to visit the tomb of St William at the east end of the nave. The crossing area, close to the saint's tomb, was to become one of the most popular places of burial in the medieval Minster, and the tomb remained a place of pilgrimage even after the removal of the saint's body to a shrine behind the high altar in 1284. Archbishop de Gray took personal advantage of the passage of pilgrims through the south portal on their way to William's tomb. In 1241 he founded a chantry for the souls

ABOVE LEFT
13 In 1255 Archbishop
Gray was buried under
a shrine-like tomb in the
chapel of St Michael in
the south transept

ABOVE RIGHT
14 Surviving grisaille
of c.1240 (s26)

of himself and his predecessors and successors in the chapel of St Michael in its eastern
aisle and in 1255 was buried there, in a shrine-like tomb. He was soon accompanied by
his successors, Sewall de Bovill (d.1258), Godfrey de Ludham (d.1266) and deans Roger
de Insula (d.1235) and Walter de Langton (d.1279), creating something of a clerical
mausoleum in the south transept.

The master mason responsible for the new transepts combined features of
northern and southern English Gothic, creating a highly textured architectural
surface. Contrasting effects of light and dark were introduced by the extensive use
of dark shafts of Purbeck marble. While the south transept façade has a large doorway
and was altered in the course of construction to accommodate a rose window, the
north façade, facing the area of the Close reserved for clerical residences, has no
major portal (12) and is dominated by the five great lancet windows known as the
Five Sisters. It is this great expanse of glass that would have confronted the pilgrim
entering by the south door.

What, then, of the glazing of the transepts? We have seen how the choir and
probably the nave had been filled with richly coloured figured panels framed by deep
borders filling the entire width of the windows with glowing colour. The stained
glass of the transept windows was strikingly different and in the latest fashion. The
eastern chapels retain no thirteenth-century glass, but the Five Sisters (n16) and two
panels in the western aisle of the south transept (s25 and s26) give an impression

of the impact of the original glazing. Above all, a high level of light was admitted, bathing the textured wall surfaces. The contrasting light and dark accents of the architecture were echoed in the windows, which were filled with grisaille glass, white glass cut into intricate shapes and decorated with trails of stylized painted foliage. The panels in s25 and s26 are much disturbed (14), and are simpler in form, perhaps reflecting their earlier date (*c*.1240?) and less prominent location. The Five Sisters, probably glazed *c*.1250, contain the more inventive and sophisticated patterns.

The full impact of the grisaille of the Five Sisters is sadly diminished by the effects of dirt, corrosion and the introduction of mending leads. In 1847 the Minster historian John Browne published coloured drawings illustrating all five of these sophisticated designs (15 and 16), revealing their original splendour. Compared, for example, to grisaille glass of similar date at Lincoln, the Five Sisters grisaille is characterized by a sinuous quality. A structure is supplied by the overlying cusped geometric shapes, picked out in blue and red glass, with smaller quantities of green and yellow. The foliage, painted in bold, expressive brush strokes, depicts a variety of leaf forms, together with clusters of fruit, enclosed within beaded borders. The cross-hatched backgrounds are characteristic of grisaille glass made in the first three-quarters of the thirteenth century. In the last quarter of the century clearer, lighter grisaille types with unpainted backgrounds became more popular.

Although the glaziers were working predominantly with white glass, a cheaper material than the imported coloured glass which is used relatively sparingly in these windows, it would be a mistake to regard them as 'cheap' windows. The repetition of five basic designs through the full height of each light would have cut down on the cartooning required, but the skilled cutting, painting and leading of these enormous windows represent a considerable glazing achievement. The grandeur of these sparkling lancets can still be appreciated on a sunny day and their impact on the thirteenth-century pilgrim can easily be imagined.

15 and 16 John Browne's nineteenth-century drawings perhaps give the best impression of the quality of the design and execution of the grisaille filling the five lancets of the Five Sisters (n16)

The Chapter House and its Vestibule

It is in the Chapter House, with its seven large five-light windows, that stained glass was first fully exploited in the Minster. The chapter house at York is in many ways the culmination of English Chapter House design – its octagonal form (18) has dispensed with the central column that characterizes the two buildings that it otherwise most closely resembles, the chapter houses of Westminster Abbey (complete by 1254) and Salisbury Cathedral (complete by c.1270). No documents referring to the building of the Chapter House or the glazing of its windows have survived. The somewhat awkward way in which the door to the vestibule cuts through the architecture of the north-east corner of the north transept, cleverly disguised though it is, suggests that the builders of the transepts had no plans for such a structure and that some years had elapsed between the two building campaigns. Comparisons with other buildings of the period suggest that the Chapter House itself was built in the 1280s, with the vestibule constructed almost immediately thereafter. By 1289 the reconstruction of the nave was being contemplated and by 1291 had been begun, by which time Chapter House and vestibule are likely to have been substantially complete. Indeed, in 1286 Archbishop Romeyn was able to declare his intention of holding a visitation in the Chapter House and it was certainly complete by 1296 when it was the venue for a meeting of Parliament. Although it cannot be assumed

LEFT
17 The martyrdom of St Thomas, framed by a simple architectural canopy, c.1290 (CHs4)

OPPOSITE
18 The interior of the Chapter House

that the stained glass had been installed by this time, heraldic and stylistic evidence suggests that the windows of the Chapter House were glazed *c*.1290, with the vestibule windows installed shortly afterwards.

The Chapter House windows established a new approach to stained glass design. The windows are 'band windows' in which light grisaille and coloured figured panels alternate in horizontal rows. The glaziers thus successfully illuminated the building, used on a daily basis for the transaction of Chapter business and from time to time for great matters of State, without sacrificing the windows as a vehicle for story-telling. This horizontal banding became the standard approach to window design in the closing years of the thirteenth century.

The figured panels in the Chapter House windows (20), with the exception of one light of window s4, are enclosed in quatrefoil frames. Similar quatrefoils appear in stained glass of *c*.1280 at La Trinité in Fécamp (Normandy), in glass from the Dominican church in Cologne of *c*.1285 (now in the cathedral) and on the embroidered Clare chasuble of *c*.1284 (in the Victoria & Albert Museum). By the last decade of the thirteenth century, such medallions had been largely superseded in stained glass by simple architectural canopies, notably in the band windows of Merton College Chapel in Oxford, dated *c*.1294. The Merton canopies, however, are significantly more developed than the rudimentary ones framing the figure scenes in Chapter House window s4 (17) . The canopy rather than the quatrefoil frame is used throughout the vestibule, being ideally suited to the tall, narrow proportions of the window openings.

The grisaille panels in the Chapter House are also of considerable interest and importance (19). Although a great deal of the architectural sculpture is still conventionalized 'stiff-leaf', the foliage in the stained glass is naturalistic. Recognizable leaf forms (maple, oak and ivy) spring from a central vertical stem growing out of the mouth of a dragon at the base of each light. A similar device is used in the earliest windows of the nave. Geometric patterns are still, however, carried in the leading patterns. Borders are narrow, and filled with climbing foliage winding around a vertical shaft.

The Chapter House windows are also notable for their display of heraldry. All seven windows of the Chapter House contain shields of arms in their tracery lights (21), and heraldry also appears in some of the vestibule windows. Heraldry became conspicuous in architectural decoration and stained glass in the second half of the thirteenth century, the period in which the formal armorial roll was evolving to record those participating in great gatherings of State or military campaigns. Henry III, for example, ordered armorial stained glass in great quantities, and although many shields of arms seem obscure to the modern visitor, their message would have been comprehensible to the medieval eye. The inclusion of a shield in a window was a means of acknowledging a benefaction or an allegiance, and it is likely that the shields in the Minster's windows were intended either to commemorate or

ABOVE
19 The painted foliage in the Chapter House windows of *c*.1290 depicts recognizable leaf and flower forms that appear to grow out of the mouths of mythical beasts. Drawing by John Browne, 1847

OPPOSITE
20 St Peter in prison, *c*.1290 (CHs2)

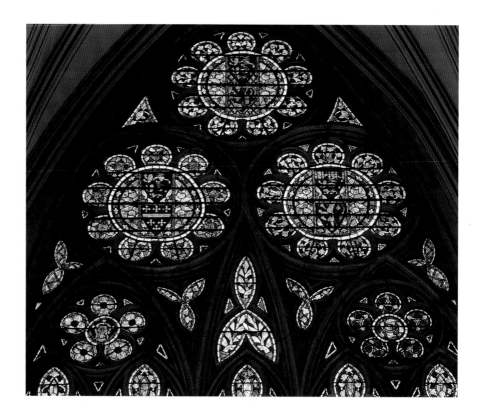

21 The tracery of each Chapter House window contains the heraldry of the king and his nobility. In the restored east window, the arms of King Edward I are accompanied by those of the Earl Marshal, the Earl of Lancaster, the Earl of Warwick and the Bulmer family

to flatter the temporal lords whose generosity was essential to the success of the Chapter's architectural projects. This is the earliest heraldic display in the Minster, and one which is dominated by the arms of the King.

The damage sustained by the Chapter House windows in the seventeenth century during the Civil War, and the replacement of some of the shields in the eighteenth century, make any interpretation of the precise meaning of the armorial display in the glass somewhat speculative. It is likely, however, that the windows acknowledge gifts made to the fabric fund, perhaps even gifts made specifically for the glazing. The heraldry is helpful in confirming the date by which the building was complete and refers to King Edward I (d.1307) and his court. Edward's arms (gules, three lions passant guardant or) appear thirteen times. The second most frequently depicted arms are those of the King's brother, Edmund ('Crouchback'), Earl of Lancaster, who died in 1296. The presence of another shield of arms, that of John Balliol (in CHs3), places the glass before 1292. In that year Balliol was crowned as King of Scotland and would have adopted the Scottish royal arms. By 1296 he had renounced his fealty to Edward I and waged war on England. Thereafter his arms would hardly have seemed appropriate for inclusion in the Chapter House windows.

The windows of the Chapter House commemorate the saints most important in the devotional life of the Minster. Some of them had an almost universal appeal in the Middle Ages, although three – St Peter, St Paul and St William – were of especial significance to the Minster. The choice of subject matter for the Chapter House windows would have rested with the Chapter and in a number of instances there is reason to believe that the personal devotional preferences of the canons may have played a part. Until the restoration of 1844–5 the east window was filled with

RIGHT
22 The funeral of the Virgin Mary, *c.*1290 (CHn2)

BELOW
23 St Paul escaping from Damascus in a basket, *c.*1290 (CHs3)

thirteenth-century scenes of Christ's Passion and Resurrection. The nineteenth-century restorers replaced the medieval panels with accurate copies (98), and the medieval glass has since disappeared. In 1959 the nineteenth-century panels were removed from the east window and installed in the nave clerestory, to be replaced in turn by a collection of fifteenth and early sixteenth-century panels which have disrupted the iconographic and stylistic consistency of the Chapter House glazing.

The Passion window, probably the first to be glazed, was flanked by windows dedicated to the Virgin Mary (22) (CHn2) and St Peter (20) (CHs2), St William (CHn3) and St Paul (23) (CHs3) and St Catherine (CHn4). In window CHs4 the mould of a single window for a single saint is broken and five saints are commemorated, one per light; St Thomas Becket (17), St Margaret, St Nicholas of Myra, St John the Baptist (24) and St Edmund, King and Martyr. A window dedicated to Christ's Passion and one honouring the Virgin Mary, depicting her part

24 Salome and Herodias with the head of St John the Baptist, c.1290 (CHs4)

in Christ's infancy and the events surrounding her death, funeral and assumption would be automatic choices in any great glazing scheme. The Cathedral is dedicated to St Peter, the subject of window CHs2. St Paul (CHs3) is frequently paired with St Peter and appears with him on the archiepiscopal seal from the time of Walter de Gray (1215–55) onwards. St William (CHn3) had been canonized in 1227, but his cult received further promotion at the time of the translation of his body to a new shrine behind the high altar in 1284, an event attended by the King. Altars and chantries dedicated to a number of the other saints in the windows attracted personal benefactions from members of the late thirteenth-century Chapter: Gilbert de Sarum, sub-dean, had founded a chantry c.1285 at the altar of St Catherine, the subject of CHn4. St Nicholas (CHs4) was honoured by William (later Archbishop) Greenfield, who by 1287 was prebendary of Laughton. The altar of St Thomas Becket, honoured in CHs4, was at the north-west crossing pier at which Precentor Peter de Ros (1289–1312) founded a chantry.

The Chapter House windows suffered some damage in the seventeenth century, probably during the Civil War, and some repairs had already taken place by 1658. Both stained glass and architectural sculpture have been more seriously damaged on the north side than on the south – perhaps as Puritan iconoclasts moved round the building from left (north) to right (south), losing enthusiasm for their work as they went. Subsequent deterioration and restoration in the nineteenth century have taken their toll and the windows are in some instances difficult to decipher as a result of paint loss, heavy mending leads and general disturbance. None the less, the vigorous painting style and the simple but effective compositions stand out. The figures are short and almost doll-like, silhouetted against the rich colour of the backgrounds. Heads are large, with simply painted but expressive features, easily legible from the ground. These characteristics can still be appreciated in the best-preserved panels, such as the death and funeral of the Virgin Mary (CHn2), St Peter in prison (CHs2), St Paul's escape from Damascus (CHs3) and the martyrdom of St Thomas Becket (CHs4).

The modern visitor to the Chapter House now sees colour only in the windows. In the Middle Ages, however, the Chapter House was one of the most colourful and richly decorated parts of the Minster. The exuberantly carved canopies overhanging the canonical stalls were coloured and gilded. The original wooden vault, removed in 1798, was painted with a scheme that complemented and extended that of the windows. Fanciful drolleries and grotesques, heraldic devices and decorative motifs accompanied large-scale figures of saints and angels that occupied the most prominent vault webs attached to the vault shafts between each window. Most of the figures can be identified from Torr's description and echo the subjects of the windows: St Peter, St Paul, St William(?), St Edmund, St John the Baptist and St Catherine were accompanied by Moses, St Mary Magdalene and the allegorical figures of Synagogue (25) and Ecclesia. An unidentified female saint probably represented St Margaret who so often accompanies St Catherine, as in window CHs4. The figure of Synagogue and upper halves of St Edmund and St William have been preserved.

25 The allegorical figure of Synagogue from the vault of the Chapter House, removed c.1798

Probably by the same workshop as the vault paintings were the life-size figures of what Torr described as 'archbishops and princes' painted in two superimposed tiers in the blind window tracery above the door. In the disposition of figures one above another, the painters anticipated the development of later stained glass design in the nave and choir, although the figures, set against diaper backgrounds, are not framed by architectural canopies. Their attributes are insufficiently specific to allow them to be identified, but Wilfrid, Paulinus, John of Beverley, William, Thomas of Bayeux, Roger of Pont L'Eveque and Walter de Gray would all have been candidates for a depiction in any commemoration of significant historical benefactors together with the mythical Ulph and Kings Edwin, Oswald and even Henry III. The later windows of the nave and choir display a similar interest in historical figures from York's past, a preoccupation reflected in the late fourteenth-century historical tables of the Vicars Choral.

Immediately above the Chapter House door are thirteen small architectural niches, reminiscent in scale of goldsmiths' work. These once contained stone statues of Christ and the twelve apostles, probably painted to resemble precious metals. A comparison with metalwork is perhaps not too fanciful, for in its pristine state the Chapter House interior would have resembled the interior of a jewelled casket, a reliquary in which members of the Chapter could

26 Joseph Halfpenny's view of the Chapter House interior as it looked c.1795, when painted glass, painted vault and painted wall survived largely intact

contemplate the life and redemptive Passion of Christ, the sanctity of his mother, the lives and miracles of the saints most revered by the Minster and the souls of its greatest benefactors.

Images and ideas first expressed on the vault and in the blind tracery over the Chapter House door recur in the windows in the vestibule that lie beyond it. Images of Synagogue and Ecclesia, for example, reappear in vestibule window CHs6. The tall, narrow windows of the vestibule take full advantage of the figure and canopy formula used experimentally inside the Chapter House (in CHs4), while the idea of placing one tier of figures above another, as in the blind tracery, is also developed. Archbishops and kings, and a display of heraldry were all significant aspects of the decoration of the vestibule; in windows CHn7 and CHs7 heraldry has moved down from the tracery into the main lights of the windows.

The disturbance of the windows by later restorers and problems in identifying all the figures make the existence of an overall, coherent theme difficult to establish. It is clear, however, that a number of windows express some of the ideological themes increasingly preoccupying the court of Edward I. In 1291 Edward began to gather evidence to substantiate his claim to overlordship of Scotland and his right to arbitrate in the disputed succession, and these preoccupations made themselves felt in York, which from 1298 became the headquarters of the Exchequer and the administration of the Scottish campaigns. Vestibule window CHn8 contains images of kings and queens (27), unidentified, but probably intended to represent Edward I, Queen Eleanor (d.1290), and their predecessors. The adjoining window (CHn9) contains saintly Kings of England, including Edward the Confessor, Oswald and probably St Edmund. Edward I had a particular devotion to Edmund and images of both Edmund and Edward the Confessor were depicted on banners carried into battle in Scotland. In design these two windows also bear a significant resemblance to a group of tiles in the British Museum depicting a king, a queen and an archbishop made in the 1290s, possibly for the ambulatory pavement near Queen Eleanor's tomb in Westminster Abbey.

The saintly kings on one side of the vestibule were matched by saintly clerics in window CHs5. Four deacon saints (28) stand above four bishops or archbishops. St Edmund Rich of Canterbury is one of the archbishops and the other could well be St Thomas Becket. One bishop cannot be identified, while the other is labelled 'S. [R]obert', perhaps for Robert Grosseteste, Bishop of Lincoln, whose canonization was unsuccessfully sought, in 1261, 1285, 1288 and 1307. One of his most active promoters was Archbishop John Romeyn of York (1286–96), a former Precentor of Lincoln. It was under Archbishop Romeyn's guidance that the next phase of the Minster's building, history unfolded.

ABOVE
27 King Edward I (?) and
Queen Philippa of France
(?) in vestibule window,
*c.*1290 (cHs5)

RIGHT
28 Two of the deacon
deacon saints in vestibule
window, *c.*1290 (CHs5)

The Nave

In 1289 preparations began for the replacement of Archbishop Thomas's eleventh-century nave. References to the ruinous and prostrate condition of the old nave are likely to have been exaggerated, but in December of that year the buildings of St Peter's school on the south side of the nave were cleared away to make room for the greater width of the new building, which was to have aisles on both sides. On 6 April 1291 Archbishop John Romeyn (1286–96) was able to lay the foundation stone of the new nave at its south-east corner, although it is likely that by this time the foundations for the new aisle walls had been prepared.

Progress on the new building was initially swift; the main arcade rests on the foundations of the outer walls of the exceptionally well-built Norman nave, saving the masons a considerable amount of preparatory work. By 1300 the area around St William's tomb at the east end of the nave was in use and by c.1315 the two aisles had been completed (30). Archbishop Romeyn was a Paris-trained theologian and it is therefore unsurprising that the new building, with its flat wall surface, slender proportions and large traceried windows has been described by Christopher Wilson in his monograph on the architecture of the Gothic cathedral (1990) as 'England's only whole-hearted essay in Rayonnant great church architecture'. Rayonnant motifs had already appeared in the Chapter House vestibule, built by some of the same masons who now worked in the nave. In the nave, however, decorative anomalies

LEFT
29 The arms of King Edward I (d.1307) and his brother, Edmund Crouchback, Earl of Lancaster (d.1296) appear in the first bay of the south nave arcade

OPPOSITE
30 The design of the nave of York Minster, begun in 1291, reveals a thorough familiarity with French architecture of the late thirteenth century

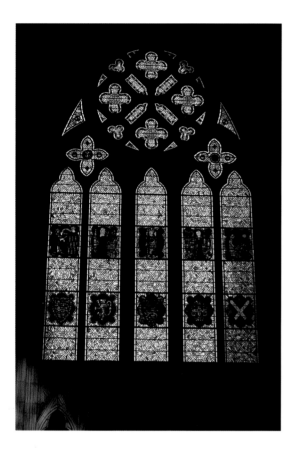

31 Nave clerestory window N21 combines early fourteenth-century heraldry and figure panels with salvaged twelfth-century grisaille

have been resolved and the Rayonnant elevation has been fully understood; the clerestory passage is pushed outside, making the clerestory windows flush with the wall. Their mullions are continued down to the triforium storey below, linking all the elements of the wall in an elegant and lofty composition. Externally, the gables over the aisle windows and the niches decorating the buttresses intended to support flying buttresses are all features with parallels in France. Not all motifs can be attributed to France, however. The tracery pattern of the clerestory windows (31) is indebted to a German source, for an almost identical pattern was used on the choir stalls of Cologne cathedral of c.1308. Other features suggest a familiarity with the King's works; heraldic shields in the arcade spandrels (29) are derived from Westminster Abbey, while figures on the external parapets are found in a Yorkshire context at Middleham Castle, but also on the royal castles of Caernarvon and Chepstow.

The aisle windows

Archbishop Romeyn did not live to see the nave completed. His successor, William Greenfield (1304–15), was to be a generous and enthusiastic promoter of the project. He made a number of gifts to the fabric and in 1306 encouraged others to do so by issuing an Indulgence worth 40 days' release from Purgatory for anyone who contributed. This Indulgence may have been intended to attract donors for the glazing of the new nave, and Archbishop Greenfield led by example, donating the first window on the south side (s29), where work had begun in 1291, depicting the life of St Nicholas of Myra (33), to whom the archbishop had a particular devotion. In 1315 he was buried beneath a splendid tomb in the chapel of St Nicholas in the north transept.

The equivalent window in the north aisle (n23) was given by Peter de Dene (32), canon of York 1312–22, the Archbishop's Chaplain and Chancellor and his Vicar General in 1309, 1312 and 1313. The window depicts the life and miracles of St Catherine (34), the patron saint of scholars and philosophers and therefore an appropriate choice for a doctor of Canon and Civil Law. The window is also remarkable for its heraldic detail, with shields of arms set in grisaille and with the tiny figures of knights and queens with heraldic tunics and gowns in the canopies and borders (35). The heraldry reflects Peter de Dene's career in the royal service of Edward I where he rubbed shoulders with the highest in the land. He came to York as a member of Archbishop Greenfield's household, although the Archbishop did not secure a place in Chapter for him until 1312. He remained a canon until 1322 and was still alive in 1332, although under Greenfield's successor, Archbishop Melton, he did not enjoy his former prominence in Minster affairs.

The inclusion of the arms of the Knights Templar in the window suggests that it was made not long after Peter de Dene's arrival in York in 1307, perhaps in response to the Archbishop's Indulgence. Although the Order was not finally dissolved until 1312, in August 1308 the Pope issued three bulls against them, accusing them of

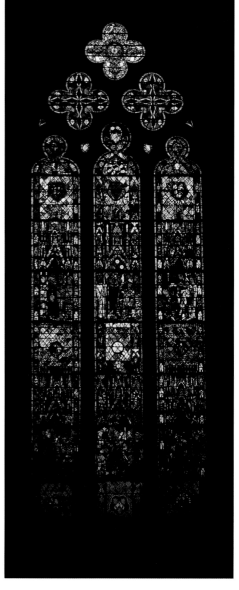

ABOVE LEFT
32 A donor 'portrait' of Peter de Dene in the 'heraldic window' of *c.*1307–8 (n23)

ABOVE
33 Archbishop Greenfield's window (s29) is dedicated to the life of St Nicholas of Myra. The Archbishop was buried in St Nicholas's chapel in 1315

LEFT
34 The main subject of the 'heraldic window' is the life of St Catherine. Here she disputes with the Emperor Maxentius, who is counselled by a green demon perched on his shoulder

heresy. Archbishop Greenfield was required to implement this policy in the northern province and the contents of the papal bulls had no doubt reached York by the end of 1308. In 1309 their lands in the north were sequestrated. Peter de Dene, a member of the Archbishop's immediate household, must have been aware of the Order's imminent fate and is unlikely to have included a reference to them in his window once this was known.

Peter de Dene's window contains what is probably the earliest use in England of yellow stain, a technique that was to revolutionize stained glass. A liquid solution of silver nitrate or sulphide was applied to the exterior surface of white glass in those areas where yellow colour was required. When fired, a stain varying from pale yellow to deep amber was achieved. This technique could be used to colour hair, beards or small-scale decorative or architectural details without recourse to the laborious process of cutting and leading-in coloured inserts. It was less commonly used on blue glass to achieve green.

Closely related to the windows given by Archbishop Greenfield and Peter de Dene are the next two windows in the south aisle of the nave (s30 and s31). The identity of the donor of window s30 cannot now be identified with certainty and its subject-matter has been confused by the intrusion of alien panels in the seventeenth century and by further restoration in the nineteenth and twentieth centuries. It may once have depicted the life of Christ. The next window, s31, dedicated to St John the Evangelist, was the gift of Chancellor Robert de Riplingham (1297–1332), about whom little is otherwise known. His name was recorded by James Torr. The Chancellor was next in dignity to the Dean and it has been suggested that the preceding window (s30) may therefore have been the gift of Dean William de Hambleton (1298–1307). On stylistic grounds the fourth window (36) on the south side (s32) also appears to belong to this group, although very little original glass survived the 1903 restoration by the firm of Burlison & Grylls. It is none the less an outstanding window. The donor was Stephen de Mauley, Archdeacon of Cleveland until his death in 1317, who was also a member of one the region's most prominent baronial families, the Mauleys of Mulgrave, near Doncaster. The window depicts the martyrdom of Saints Stephen, Andrew and John the Baptist in its upper register, although it is the depiction of six members of the family that has the greatest impact (38). Stephen de Mauley is accompanied by his father, Peter, Lord Mauley (d.1279) and his four brothers, Peter, Lord Mauley (d.1308), Sir Edmund (steward of Edward II's household, d.1314), Sir John (d. 1331) and Sir Robert (d.1331). Two of the saints, Stephen and John, are the name-saints of the lords below. Each figure holds aloft his shield of arms and the Mauley

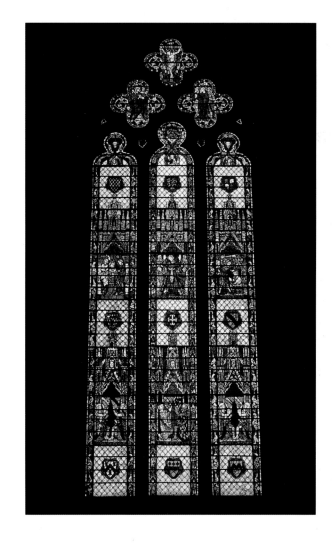

ABOVE

37 Richard Tunnoc (d.1330),
goldsmith, bell-founder and
Mayor of York, commemorated
with St William and images of
his own profession (n24)

LEFT

38 Stephen de Mauley,
Archdeacon of Richmond
(d.1317) accompanied by his
father Peter (d.1279)

OPPOSITE

39 The martyrdom of St Peter
from the Penancer's window

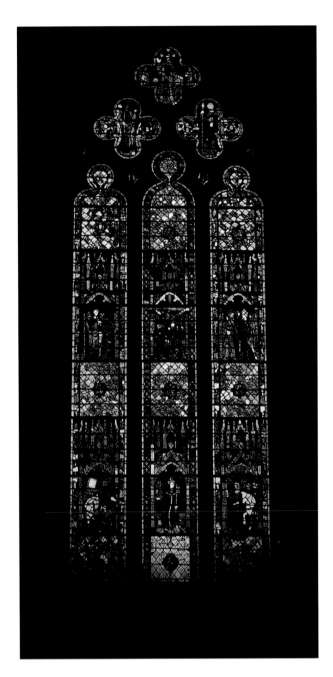

arms appear again in the stone shields in the south nave arcade and the clerestory windows above. The remaining windows on the south side have suffered much damage and disturbance and the westernmost windows on both north and south sides had lost their medieval glazing by the seventeenth century.

The glaziers responsible for the group of windows commissioned by senior members of the Minster clergy and destined for the south aisle of the nave (s29–s31), together with window n23, worked in very similar styles and may have belonged to a single workshop. In the windows of the north aisle other workshops can be identified. Window n24, to the west of Peter de Dene's heraldic window, is in marked contrast to it in both style and content. While the 'Heraldic Window' gives a glimpse of a cosmopolitan, courtly world and commemorates a saint of universal significance, Richard Tunnoc's window (37), with its scenes of bell-founding, depicts the preoccupations of a wealthy York craftsman, and commemorates St William, a saint whose popularity was never great outside York. Tunnoc was a goldsmith and bailiff of the city 1320–1 and mayor in 1327. In the following year he founded a chantry at the altar of St Thomas Becket, one of only three private citizens to found a chantry in the medieval Minster, and who, unusually, chose to be buried there in 1330 rather than in his parish church.

By the same glaziers is the window depicting the activities of the Penancers (n27), the Minster clerics appointed by the Archbishop to hear the confessions of the Chapter and those of such eminence that they did not wish to confess to their parish clergy. In 1308 William Langtoft was appointed to the post and in 1311 was specifically entrusted with the task of hearing the confessions of the Templars, who thanks to Greenfield's moderation,

41 The Pilgrimage
window, c.1325 (n25)

PREVIOUS PAGES
40 A Penancer of the
Minster (n27). The
window was probably
the gift of William
Langtoft, who was
appointed in 1308
and died in 1321

escaped torture and death, a common fate elsewhere in Europe. Langtoft was also one of the keepers of the fabric, and in 1312 Greenfield entrusted 100 marks to his custody. While the main scenes in the lower register depict the Penancers at their penancing (40), the borders show tonsured clerics holding keys and pouring coins into coffers and masons hewing stone, apparently reflecting the various aspects of Langtoft's career. In the upper register the martyrdom of St Paul (with the unusual scene of Drusiana blindfolding the saint) and St Peter is depicted (39). The seated Christ in Majesty does not belong in the window; in the seventeenth century Torr saw a clerical figure in this position. In the early years of this century J. W. Knowles recorded part of what seems to have been part of Langtoft's name under one of the scenes of penance. If Langtoft was indeed connected with the provision of the window, the lost clerical saint might have been St William, so often linked with Peter and Paul in York devotions and also Langtoft's name saint, or even Thomas Becket, another victim of martyrdom, at whose altar Langtoft founded a chantry in 1317 and where he was buried in 1321.

The remaining two windows in the north aisle containing original glass are also of considerable interest. The so-called Pilgrimage window (41) (n25) depicts the Crucifixion in its upper panels, while in its lower register is a large image of St Peter, flanked by a male and female pilgrim. It is the borders of the window that have attracted the greatest interest, for in their treatment they resemble the page of an illuminated manuscript.

The vertical borders contain squirrels and monkeys with urine flasks, a parody of the medical profession, while along the base of the window (42) is Renard the fox preaching to a cock, a parody of the funeral of the Virgin Mary enacted by monkeys, a monkey doctor examining a patient, a parody of a hunt and the famous scene of Renard stealing a goose. These amusing and irreverent scenes can be compared to some of the sculpted scenes in the nave and to manuscript pages of the period.

Immediately west is the Martyrdom window (n26), depicting the martyrdom of St Lawrence, St Denis and St Vincent in its upper register with the martyrdom theme carried into the small medallions in the grisaille panels (St Edmund and St Stephen), with St Peter and St Paul in the tracery above. A donor figure in the lower register is accompanied by an inscription requesting prayers for Vincent, whose name-saint appears above. Two unidentifed donor figures appear in the third light. The borders of the window are filled with the alternating arms of Mowbray (gules a lion rampant argent) and Clare (or three chevrons gules), presumably a reference to John, second Lord Mowbray and grandson of Rose Clare, sister of Gilbert, the last Clare earl of Gloucester, who died at Bannockburn (1314). John was Governor of York and custos of Galtres Forest in 1312 and his arms appear in glass in clerestory window N21 and in stone in the seventh bay of the south nave arcade. The window is likely to date from before 1322, when John was executed for treason after the battle of Boroughbridge. It may be John and his wife Alina (de Braose) who appear in the window with Vincent.

42 The borders of the Pilgrimage window resemble the margins of an illuminated manuscript in which human activities are parodied by animals. The so-called 'monkey's funeral' is a parody of the funeral of the Virgin Mary

The heraldry

While the reconstruction of the nave was initiated and supported by the Archbishop and the Chapter, the project undoubtedly benefited from the transformation of York into the second city of the realm by the presence of the Exchequer and the military administration for long periods between 1298 and 1338. The nave arcade is decorated with a series of great stone shields commemorating the King and members of the nobility in a display that resembles both that in the nave aisles of Westminster Abbey and the armorial rolls that recorded those gathered together for parliaments, council and military action. The sequence of shields commences with the arms of Edward I and his brother, Edmund, Earl of Lancaster (d.1296), which are carved in the spandrels of the first bay of the south nave arcade (29). The King had assisted at the translation of the relics of St William in 1284, and had made offerings at the shrine and tomb in 1300 and it is likely that he had contributed to the costs of the work. A similar heraldic display is found in the clerestory windows, in each of which are the arms of the King flanked by four shields of arms of noble families who owed him military and political service. The shields probably represent contributions to the fabric fund. Bishop Anthony Bek, whose arms appear in the window N21 (43) and in the second bay of the south arcade, had funded the translation of St William and the construction of the new shrine. The Percy and Vavasour families, whose arms appear in stone in the seventh and eighth bays of the arcade, were both donors of building materials. In 1313 Peter de Mauley (d.1348), whose family arms are well represented in the nave, was required to pay a fine of 100 marks to the fabric fund as punishment for adultery. It must be assumed that other contributions were of a more voluntary nature!

43 This shield in N21 commemorates Bishop Anthony Bek of Durham (d.1311), who in 1284 paid for the translation of St William's relics from the nave to a new shrine in the choir

Some of the individuals commemorated were long-lived and could have contributed to the fabric fund at any time over a long period. Sir Ralph Bulmer, for example, whose arms appear in glass in window N24 and in stone in bay 5 of the north nave arcade, succeeded to his estates in 1299 and lived until 1356. Sir Henry Fitzhugh (S27), who succeeded his father in 1305, also died in 1356. On the other hand, three of those commemorated in the nave died at the calamitous battle of Bannockburn in 1314; Gilbert de Clare, the last Earl of Gloucester (bay 2 of the south nave arcade and window S22), Sir Robert de Clifford (S25) and Sir Edmund Mauley (S23 and nave aisle window s32). Two of those represented (Sir John Mowbray, N21 and the seventh bay of the south nave arcade, and Sir Robert Ryther in S27) were executed for treason after the battle of Boroughbridge in 1322, while others represented were discredited adherents of Thomas of Lancaster who escaped death but are unlikely to have been chosen for commemoration by a loyal Dean and Chapter.

Although the nave heraldry does not allow precise bay-by-bay dating, closer scrutiny of the careers of individual knights and barons represented in the nave in glass and stone suggests that one period above all was auspicious for donations. Nearly all were prominent in the prosecution of Edward I's Scottish campaigns of

1298–1307. A large number of the shields in the nave are also found in the Falkirk Roll recording those involved in the triumphant Falkirk campaign of 1298, for example. Most of the nobles represented were called upon to serve in person, as landowners in the north and Scottish marches, and a number were to be severely impoverished as a result of Edward II's failure to maintain the status quo after his father's death.

Many of these men were also bound together by ties of fealty and family, the latter most commonly represented by intermarriage. Sir Ralph Bulmer and Sir Nicholas de Meynill, for example, held lands of Peter de Mauley while Bulmer also held land of Ralph de Neville. Sir William de Ryther married the daughter of Robert, Lord Ros of Helmsley. Sir Peter de Mauley (IV) married one daughter of Sir Thomas Furnival and committed adultery with her sister. Sir Ralph Bulmer and Sir Henry FitzHugh were brothers in law, and Sir Ralph married Sir Walter de Fauconberg's widow. Walter de Fauconberg's son, also Walter, had married a daughter of Sir Robert de Ros of Helmsley, but predeceased his father, another casualty of Bannockburn. The nave is thus a microcosm of a relatively small and close-knit aristocratic society.

There is also a sense in which the Minster's nave presents a complex image in glass and stone of a perfect society of knightly amity and loyalty, led by the King and blessed by the Church. A similar image had been perpetuated in the earlier nave of Westminster Abbey. In both instances, however, this image was a fiction. The later years of Edward I's reign were marred by friction between sovereign and nobility, tensions that greatly worsened after 1307, during the reign of his politically inept son. Success against the Scots in the opening decade of the fourteenth century perhaps camouflaged these social and political fissures, but the disaster at Bannockburn reopened the wounds and heralded a period of violence and unrest in the north which had a serious impact on the material prosperity of the northern province. Dissatisfaction with the King and his rapacious favourites finally erupted into open rebellion. Thomas of Lancaster was executed in Pontefract, but a number of his supporters, some of whom had contributed to the Minster's fabric fund, were hung, drawn and quartered in York. Thus, after 1322, the concept manifested in the nave heraldry would have seemed increasingly at odds with reality.

The clerestory

The balance of alternating light and dark bands of glass established in the nave aisles is maintained at clerestory level, although in only one window (N25) are simple canopies preferred to the earlier type of medallion frame. Light levels were maintained by the panels of reused twelfth-century unpainted geometric grisaille, extended and adapted to receive two registers of coloured glass. The lower coloured register in each window was filled with the shields of arms discussed above. The upper register was filled with a mixture of reused

44 In nave clerestory window N25 simple canopies frame the figure scenes. St Agnes holds the martyr's palm

twelfth-century glass and newly made figure panels. The Romanesque glass has been discussed fully above, but the nature of its reuse sheds valuable light on the progress of the fourteenth-century work in the nave.

The original location in the nave clerestory of the reused panels has been affected by nineteenth-century restoration and by the introduction into the two easternmost windows on north and south sides (N19, N20, S21 and S22) of the 1844 Barnett copies of the Chapter House east window, which resulted in the shift westwards of a number of panels. It is clear, none the less, that the predominance of reused Romanesque glass was originally on the south side of the nave, with seven of the windows glazed with twelfth-century glass. Of the northern clerestory, only the first two eastern bays were glazed in this way and these bays are the ones that buttress the central tower and would thus have been constructed quickly, in tandem with the bays on the south side.

While it cannot be discounted that the Romanesque glass and sculpture was saved as a souvenir of an earlier venerable structure, it is more likely that financial expediency was the overriding motive. Both glass and stone were reused predominantly on the south side of the nave and at high levels, where their antiquity would have been less evident. At aisle level the Chapter had taken a lead in the provision of new windows. Short of funds, and unable to attract sufficient secular donors, the Chapter would seem to have dipped into its own stores for salvaged material, enabling the south side of the nave, facing the town, to be glazed quickly, and the niches of its pinnacles to be filled with sculpture.

45 The Annunciation to the Virgin Mary, one of the Joys of the Virgin depicted in N23

In the glazing of the north nave clerestory, the Chapter was more successful in attracting donors. The relationship between the workshops employed at aisle level and those who made the new clerestory windows has not been fully investigated. At first glance, the unsophisticated, almost naive figure style of the clerestory windows, with short, broadly proportioned figures with large heads and hands, simply painted, without yellow stain and on glass with a limited colour range, might prompt the conclusion that the clerestory windows are earlier in date than the more consciously elegant aisle windows. The donor of window N24 can be identified as Robert of Waynfleet, Abbot of Bardney, who resigned in 1318. The circumstances of his turbulent career suggest a date of *c*.1311 for his gift, close in date to the more sophisticated aisle windows below. This identification suggests that subjective stylistic observations must be treated with caution, and it seems likely that the relatively unsophisticated style of the clerestory windows is a response to their location. Some foreshortening and exaggeration of the figures makes them more legible from the ground. The restricted palette and absence of yellow stain was perhaps a response to the Romanesque glass that the glaziers were installing in adjoining windows, and the use of cusped medallions rather than canopies ensures that the figured panels balance the heraldic display in the lower register.

As in the aisles below, the diversity and repetition of subject-matter suggests that while the Dean and Chapter were able to insist upon a consistency of design and general layout, the subject-matter of the clerestory windows was left largely to the donor. Abbot Waynfleet chose clerical saints for window N24; St Peter, St Edmund, two archbishops (St William and St Wilfrid (?) and a bishop blessing a king (Edwin and Paulinus (?). The unidentified donor of N23 chose subjects that together represent the Joys of the Virgin Mary – the Annunciation (45), Nativity, Resurrection, Ascension and

46 One of two scenes depicting the commerce of a wine merchant in N21. Trade scenes in English stained glass are rare

Coronation. Of the less complete windows, there are three female martyrs under simple canopies (44) (N25), and figures of St James the Great and a kneeling male and female donor dressed as pilgrims at a shrine (N21). St James's shrine at Compostela was the most popular pilgrimage destination in the Middle Ages. Sir Robert Fitzwalter, for example, whose arms appear in N22, went on three pilgrimages, including one to Compostela in 1280, and in 1361 Agnes de Holme left a sum of money equivalent to the cost of one man going to Compostela for the making of a window in honour of St James. The shield held by the male pilgrim now shows a bear and led Dean Milner-White to identify the figure as Treasurer Francis Orsini (FitzUrse) and his wife. Orsini would not have been shown in secular dress, nor would he have had a wife, so this cannot be correct. Torr described the shield in question as 'or a lion passant murrey [purple]', similar to the arms of Edward I's military commander in Scotland, Henry de Lacy, Earl of Lincoln (1257–1312), whose arms were or a lion rampant purple.

Of particular interest are two scenes now in window N21, depicting the activities of a wine merchant (46). Together with Tunnoc's bell-founding (n24), these are the only images in the nave windows of York's commercial life. Images of trades and occupations are relatively rare in English stained glass (an image of an early fourteenth-century stonemason survives at Helmdon in Northamptonshire). The closest parallel to the York window is in a thirteenth-century window dedicated to St Lubin in Chartres Cathedral, which was given by the wine merchants of the city. There are no later images of trade or commerce in the Minster's windows, perhaps because by the end of the fourteenth century the performance of the Corpus Christi play cycle provided an alternative outlet for trade guild munificence, although it is impossible to tell whether these panels mark the generosity of an individual merchant or a 'corporate' donation.

The west wall

The interior of the nave is dominated by the curvilinear grace of the west window, which in both scale and design marks a departure from the treatment of the other nave windows. Although the tracery design of the west windows of the two aisles (n30 and s36) is the same as that of the rest of the nave aisles, the stained glass of these two windows links them to the west window glazing campaign. Examination of the west front of the Minster reveals that while the aisles, including windows n30 and s36, and lower stage of the west wall belongs to the first nave campaign, the upper stages of the west wall, including the tracery of the west window, were constructed in a later and stylistically separate phase. The break between one building campaign and another can be discerned most clearly at the level of the fourth tier of arcading, where nodding ogee arches are introduced into the canopy heads. This is most easily seen on the exterior. Internally, the most dramatic expression of this phase is the tracery of the west window itself.

The resumption of work on the nave c.1330, and the glazing of the west windows, can be attributed to the encouragement and personal generosity of Archbishop William Melton (1316–40). Melton is said to have contributed £20 to the making of the new tomb-shrine of St William at the east end of the nave, empty since 1284, but still a site of veneration. On 7 June 1338 he made a gift of 500 marks to the fabric fund and on 4 February 1339 gave a further 100 marks for the glazing of the west window, described as 'newly constructed'.

The original contracts for the west windows do not survive, although Torr, who saw them before their disappearance, summarized them in both Latin and English. Melton entrusted his 100 marks to the keepers of the fabric, Thomas Sampson and Thomas Ludham, and it was Thomas Ludham who, four days later, signed the contracts with the glaziers commissioned to make the west windows. Robert [Ketelbarn?] was to make the west window, while Thomas Bouesdun was to glaze n30 and s36, ordered at the same time, although under separate contract. The latter once contained donor figures, although these have been lost, replaced by figures made by William Peckitt in the eighteenth century. Torr's transcriptions of the lost medieval documents are not without their problems, but it would seem that the two contracts were framed rather differently. Thomas Bouesdun was paid 11 marks for each window, while Robert was to receive 6d per foot for white glass and 12d per foot for coloured. Painting and glazing are not mentioned separately, although an additional payment of £30 is mentioned, perhaps intended to cover these aspects of the window's manufacture. Nor do the contracts mention the subject-matter of the

windows, which must have been specified in separate documents, probably in the form of a certified sketch design (called a vidimus).

Even without the documentary evidence of Archbishop Melton's register, his involvement might have been guessed, for in the lowest tier of figures, eight of his predecessors are depicted (50). In the late seventeenth century Torr was able to distinguish six of the eight inscriptions identifying St John of Beverley (705–18), Thomas of Bayeux (1070–1100), St Wilfrid (669–77), St Oswald 972–92), St William (1143–7 and 1153–4) and Sewall de Bovill (1256–8). St Paulinus, St Chad, St Wilfrid II, St Bosa and St Egbert would all be candidates for the remaining two unidentified figures. The inclusion of Thomas of Bayeux, who was not a saint, nor even, like Sewall de Bovill, locally revered as one, is interesting, for it suggests that Melton was anxious to be identified with another great benefactor and builder of the nave. Indeed, the late fourteenth-century historical tables of the Vicars Choral commemorated him in this capacity. The window thus represents a luminous statement about the history and prestige of the northern province and its great cathedral church. The archbishops are represented as the apostles of the north and this image provides a timely antidote to the celebration of the secular nobility of the region commemorated in the main arcade and nave clerestory.

Above the bishops and archbishops stand the twelve biblical apostles (49), somewhat awkwardly squashed into eight lights. St Paul, so often paired with St Peter in York Minster, has been included at the expense of St Matthias, the apostle who replaced Judas Iscariot. The third and fourth tiers contain scenes spread across two lights, depicting five of the Joys of the Virgin Mary — the Annunciation, the Nativity (51), the Resurrection, the Ascension (52) and the Coronation of the Virgin. With the exception of the medallions of the pelican in her piety and the Agnus Dei, the tracery is filled with decorative foliage. While the west window is far richer in palette and decorative repertoire than the earlier nave windows, it none the less maintains the pattern of balanced horizontal zones of light and dark established in

OPPOSITE

49 St John the Evangelist, one of the best preserved figures in the west window, illustrating the skill with which the designer, Master Robert, has integrated the constructional lead into the design

BELOW

50 The first tier of figures in the west window depicts a group of the illustrious bishops and archbishops of the See of York, made from only three cartoons

51 The Nativity of Christ has been arranged across two lights of the west window but is linked by the architecture of the thrones. The head of St Joseph was replaced in the eighteenth century

the earlier glazing programmes. The west windows of north and south aisles depict the Virgin and Child with St Catherine and St Margaret (s36) and the Crucifixion with the Virgin and St John the Evangelist (n30). All three windows were restored in 1757–8 by William Peckitt, who supplied new heads for a number of the figures, which in terms of technique and style are somewhat incongruous.

The size of the workshops headed by Master Robert and Thomas Bouesdun is unknown. All three windows are characterized by a remarkable consistency of quality and style and are stylistically, to all intents and purposes, indistinguishable from one another. A considerable quantity of other glass in the Minster and the city's parish churches seems to be by these, or very closely related workshops. Large figures of Saints Stephen, Christopher and Lawrence now in the Lady Chapel aisle (n4) may have been made for the westernmost windows of the nave aisle (n29 and s35), while in windows n2, n5, s2, S3 (54) and S4 (53) are figures and narrative panels of unknown provenance, reused in the Lady Chapel in the late fourteenth century. Panels depicting the Annunciation (55) and Joachim in the wilderness have been inserted in nave aisle window s35. These panels, many of them executed in a delicate monochrome set off by coloured backgrounds, may have come from the chapel of St Mary and All Angels, although recently it has been suggested that the parish church of St Mary ad Valvas, a property of the Dean and Chapter situated to the east of the Lady Chapel, demolished in 1364, may have been their original home.

The west windows and the stylistically related panels scattered around the Minster provide valuable evidence of the transformation of York glass-painting in the second quarter of the fourteenth century. The glass suggests a familiarity, albeit sometimes misunderstood, of new pictorial formulae and iconographic features derived ultimately from Italian Trecento art. The kneeling angel in the Annunciation in the west window and in the panel now in window s35, and the grieving angels flying around the Crucified Christ in window s36, for example, have their origins in Italian wall and panel paintings. While direct contact with portable works of art imported from Italy cannot be completely discounted, contact with an alternative source of Italianate influence, namely Parisian art of the first quarter of the century, is more plausible. In works like the Hours of Jeanne d'Evreux and the Belleville Breviary, the Parisian miniaturist Jean Pucelle had assimilated Italian iconographic

52 A group of apostles witnesses the Ascension. One of the best-preserved figure groups in the west window

RIGHT
54 The Massacre of the Innocents, made c.1340
and reused in Lady Chapel clerestory S3

OPPOSITE
55 The Annunciation, c.1340 (s35)

BELOW
53 St Margaret and St Helen, figures made for
an unknown location, c.1340, reused c.1370 in
Lady Chapel clerestory window S4

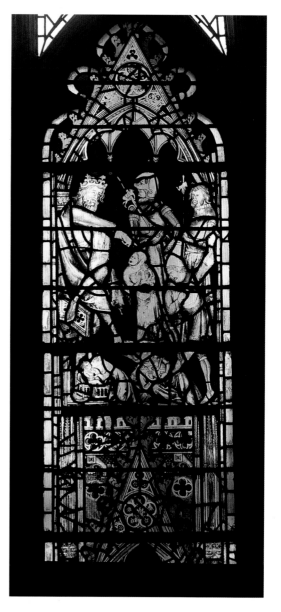

innovations and spatial experimentation with Parisian refinement and delicacy. A comparison of the 'doll's-house' interior of the Annunciation in s35 (55) with the equivalent scene in the Hours of Jeanne d'Evreux reveals the relationship between the art of Master Robert and his circle and that of Jean Pucelle and his followers, although it is also a comparison that reveals that the York glass-painter has imperfectly understood his model; the York glass panel is full of spatial inconsistencies. The preference for an essentially monochrome effect, with figures silhouetted against coloured backgrounds, enlivened only with yellow stain, is a further indication of an indebtedness to 'Pucellian' art.

In England it was episcopal patrons like Bishop Grandison of Exeter, Bishop Richard de Bury of Durham and Archbishop William Melton of York, all of whom had enjoyed careers in the service of the King, who sponsored artists who were responsible for introducing these new styles.

The Glazing of the Eastern Arm

The replacement of the cathedral's Romanesque eastern arm was achieved in two phases. The Lady Chapel (56) was constructed in the period 1361–c.1373 and the western choir was rebuilt between c.1394 and c.1420. Despite Archbishop Melton's generosity the nave remained incomplete at his death in 1340. The nave vault had not been installed, the roof lacked a lead covering so that in 1345 puddles of water were reported to be gathering on the pavement. None the less, by 1348, the Chapter was beginning to contemplate the construction of a new choir, for in that year Canon Thomas Sampson bequeathed £20 to the fabric, as long as work began on the new choir within one year.

The arrival in York of the plague known as the Black Death in the summer of 1349 offers the most likely explanation for the disruption of these plans. Nearly half of the beneficed clergy of the diocese died and it is likely that craftsmen were as badly affected as their patrons. There were to be further outbreaks in 1361 and 1369. Throughout England, architectural projects were interrupted or curtailed and stained glass production was sharply reduced. In the glazing of St Stephen's chapel, Westminster (1351–2), for example, King Edward III was forced to summon glaziers from 27 counties in order to assemble a sufficiently large work force. In York, the chantry chapel to the east of the south transept planned by Archbishop Zouche (1340–52), for which generous funds were made available, remained unfinished at the time of his death, and he was buried in the nave.

Zouche's successor, Archbishop John Thoresby (1352–73) therefore inherited a cathedral church with an incomplete and leaking nave and with unfulfilled ambitions to replace its Romanesque choir. Thoresby was an energetic administrator, reformer and educator, probably related to Archbishop Melton, to whose patronage he was indebted for advancement early in his career. He first turned his attention to the completion of the nave, in 1353 issuing an Indulgence to those giving to the fabric and in 1355 he supplied the timber which enabled the master carpenter Philip of Lincoln to complete the nave vault soon afterwards. For probably no more than a few years the Minster functioned without the distractions of builders, scaffolding and partially constructed walls. With the nave finally complete, attention soon turned east once more.

The Lady Chapel

On 30 July 1361 the foundation stone of the four-bay eastern extension to the cathedral was laid on a virgin site to the east of Archbishop Roger's choir. In his submission to the Pope, Thoresby explained his reasons for requiring the new building. The first reason was liturgical; the Minster lacked a seemly place in which to celebrate the daily mass of the Virgin Mary. The other arguments touch upon aesthetic matters; the old choir was too 'homely' and compared unfavourably to the magnificence of the newly completed nave. Furthermore, it was fitting that the church be adorned throughout with a uniform beauty and craftsmanship. Thoresby

OPPOSITE

56 The interior of the choir and Lady Chapel, dominated by the great east window, which serves as a reredos for the entire eastern arm of the Minster

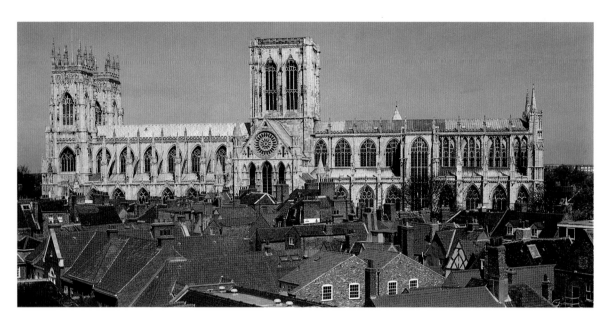

57 The eastern transepts mark the division of the two phases of the reconstruction of the eastern arm of the Minster. The Lady Chapel (extreme right) was built by Archbishop Thoresby between 1361 and c.1373, while the choir (between the eastern transepts and the crossing tower) was constructed over a longer period, between c.1394 and c.1420

was prepared to back this up with money. Over the next twelve years he was to pay £200 per year into the fabric fund and offered spiritual inducements to those who also contributed. The market for Indulgences was so valuable that steps had to be taken to suppress forgeries.

With this steady stream of money, the building progressed rapidly. By 1364 the chantries and altars at the eastern end of Archbishop Roger's choir were suspended, a prelude to the demolition of the eastern bay of the old choir. A temporary wall must have been erected on the eastern side of the choir transepts to protect the Minster from the noise, dust and disruption of work on the new structure. By the time Thoresby died, on 6 November 1373, the Lady Chapel was sufficiently complete to receive his burial before the altar. It is clear, however, that work remained to be done in the Lady Chapel. The vaults of the aisles, for example, were not inserted for another forty years. Most of the windows were unglazed and the east window remained incomplete and empty. The loss of Thoresby's enthusiastic interest and financial support resulted in a dramatic slowing down in the pace of work.

His successor, Alexander Neville (1373–88), best known for his quarrels with the Bishop of Durham, the Canons of Beverley and his own Chapter, showed little interest in his cathedral church. Little leadership could be expected from the Deanery, occupied by two absentees in the period 1366–85. Faced by a financial crisis and an absence of patronage, the works department reverted to a tried and tested solution. Salvaged stained glass from an as yet unidentified location was used to fill some of the empty clerestory windows (58). A collection of figures and narrative panels of exceptional quality, originally made c.1340, were installed in the three easternmost windows (windows S2–S4). Window S2 has since lost this glass, perhaps used to patch the east window c.1700. The 1340s glass remains in windows S3 and S4, while other panels have found their way into the north aisle. This collection has been discussed more fully above in connection with the west window.

Just as in the nave, the reused glass was sited at a high level, where its slightly old-fashioned appearance would be less noticeable. Its elevated position also protected it from the 1829 fire which did so much damage in the choir and Lady Chapel and accounts in part for the poor state of preservation of the original glazing of the Lady Chapel aisles. In windows s2 (59) and s5 are the fragmentary remains of windows probably made *c.*1373 to prepare the Lady Chapel for use. In window s5 are the heavily restored figures of St James the Great, St Edward the Confessor and St John the Evangelist (probably originally in s2) under elaborate canopies of considerable interest. In common with illuminated manuscripts associated with the Fitzwarin Psalter (Paris, Bibliotèque Nationale Ms. lat. 765), the designer has abandoned the 'bird's eye perspective' favoured in the 1330s and 1340s in favour of a three-sided superstructure topped by turrets and inhabited by figures. Side shafts are pierced with narrow lancets, wide niches contain figures and have visible vaults, angled to create the impression of projecting forms. The dormer roofs of the canopy tops are positioned diagonally to enhance perspectival effects, and barred windows, with a variety of ironwork patterns, give depth to the fictive masonry.

The windows of the north aisle appear to have been glazed at a slightly later date, reflecting the renewed impetus that followed Neville's removal and the election of Archbishop Thomas Arundell in 1388. Arundell's episcopacy coincided with the active and resident deanery of Edmund Stafford (1385–95). Arundell was a generous benefactor to his cathedral, in 1394 giving vestments, ecclesiastical vessels and a reliquary containing two thorns believed to be from the crown of thorns. He also gave the stained glass in window n5, although most of the glass itself has disappeared and the exact date of the donation is not known.

Also dating from Arundell's episcopacy are the fifteen figures of apostles and prophets in clerestory windows S5, N4 (60) and N5. The apostles hold curling ribbons with sentences of the Creed, while the prophets hold messianic texts from

58 In the years around 1370 the Lady Chapel clerestory was glazed with panels of glass originally made *c.*1340 in an attempt to complete Archbishop Thoresby's new Lady Chapel. The exterior tracery casts a shadow on the glass

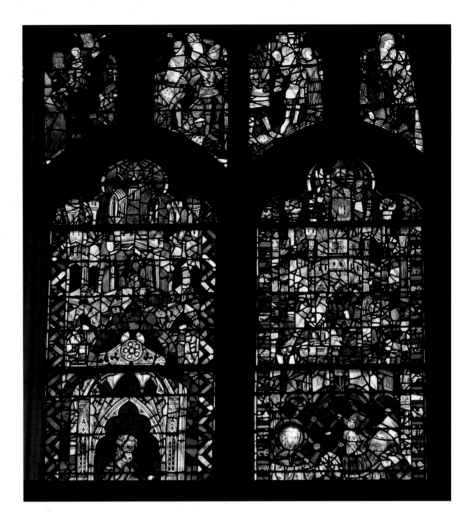

59 Very little remains of the original glazing of the Lady Chapel aisles, but these canopies in All Saints Chapel (s2) were probably made *c*.1370

OPPOSITE
60 Lady Chapel window N4, together with N5 and S5, was glazed in the 1380s with figures of the apostles and prophets holding appropriate sentences from the Creed and messianic prophecy

the Old Testament. The series must have once extended into windows N2 and N3, which together provide the additional nine lights necessary to accommodate twelve apostles and twelve prophets. That the Creed series was inserted at a later date than the reused glass in the windows on the south side of the clerestory can be deduced from the rather awkward arrangement of the series across four windows on the north side and one on the south. A more balanced arrangement of apostles on the south side and prophets on the north might have been expected.

Comparison with other glazing schemes installed in the period around 1390, notably those associated with the patronage of William of Wykeham, Bishop of Winchester and the workshop of Thomas Glazier of Oxford (New College, Oxford *c*.1385 and Winchester College *c*.1393), confirms this dating for the York Creed figures. The canopies of the York figures are remarkably similar to those at Oxford, constructed from strongly drawn three-dimensional forms, with turrets and recessed windows, although the York canopies lack the playful grotesques introduced into some of the Oxford canopies.

The figure style of the York apostles and prophets, with their softly modelled features (61 and 62) and large gesturing hands, is closest to the later stages of the New College scheme, particularly the Jesse Tree made for the west window, probably

RIGHT
61 Amos in N4, probably
the work of the Minster
glazier John Burgh and
his workshop

FAR RIGHT
62 Daniel in N4; like
Amos, he holds a ribbon
with a prophetic text on it

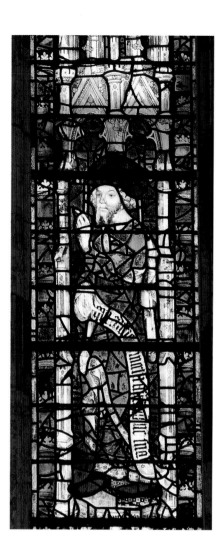

*c.*1390. This is in a noticeably softer style than the earlier antechapel figures, a style that had come to dominate the workshop of Thomas Glazier by the time the Winchester College windows were made in the early 1390s. In 1765 the York glazier William Peckitt removed the New College west window, retaining it in part payment for work done for the College. The glass was subsequently acquired for the Minster by Peckitt's patron, Dean Fountayne of York (1747–1802), and it now fills window s8 (63), allowing a close stylistic comparison with the Lady Chapel to be made with comparative ease. Similarities are not confined to style, however. Dr French has recently pointed out the close textual links between six of the prophets that the York and Oxford schemes have in common. Indeed, the parallels include textual errors apparently introduced at Oxford and repeated in York.

The windows of New College and Winchester College were in two of the most important new buildings of their day and it is quite conceivable that the York glass-painters had seen them. The relationships between the patrons involved were certainly very close. William of Wykeham had been a canon of York early in his career. Between 1386 and 1391 the post of Chancellor of England was passed back and forth between William of Wykeham and Thomas Arundell, while Edmund

63 This figure of Manasseh, made for the chapel of New College, Oxford, by Thomas Glazier of Oxford, was installed in Minster window s8 in 1785 by William Peckitt

Stafford, Dean of York, served as Keeper of the Privy Seal in 1389, becoming Chancellor in 1396, after his departure for the bishopric of Exeter. In 1397 Stafford's successor as Dean of York, Richard Clifford, became Keeper of the Privy Seal and in 1401 was succeeded in both roles by Thomas Langley, Dean of York, 1401–6. It is not difficult to envisage how the latest ideas could flow between London, Oxford, Westminster and York.

In the Minster fabric rolls, which survive with some gaps from *c.*1371 onwards, it is clear that the Minster's principal 'resident' glazier between 1399 and 1419 was John Burgh. J. A. Knowles, one of the first writers to discuss the York windows in a wider national context, speculated as to the relationship between John Burgh and William Burgh, glazier to Richard II and Henry IV. In 1402 William was commissioned to make some of the most expensive glass ever recorded, to fill windows in Henry IV's new oratory at Eltham Palace and in 1404 a John Burgh is recorded working at Eltham. Although John Burgh's work in the Lady Chapel clerestory first introduced the softly modelled style of 'International Gothic' into the Minster, the glazing of the chapel's greatest window was to be entrusted to a 'foreigner', John Thornton, a native of Coventry.

The east window

The original contract for the glazing of the east window was entered into a lost Chapter Act book covering the period 1390–1410. Fortunately, a summary of it survives in one English version and two Latin versions. In December 1405 John Thornton was commissioned to make the window within a three-year period, supplying materials and the workforce, in return for a total sum of £46, with a bonus of £10 on satisfactory completion of the window. He was to paint with his own hand those figures and scenes ordained by the Dean and Chapter. The date of completion, MCCCCVIII (1408), appears in the glass at the apex of the window.

Medieval Coventry was a major centre of glass-painting and both Archbishop Scrope (1398–1405) and Walter Skirlaw, Bishop of Durham (1388–1406), the donor of the east window, had been Bishop of Coventry and Lichfield. In January 1398 Skirlaw had been elected Archbishop of York and may have assigned the funds for the window as a thank-offering. In the event, he was set aside in favour of Richard Scrope. Skirlaw remained a generous patron of the Minster, however, for his arms appear alongside Scrope's archiepiscopal shield in the first south bay of the new choir (74) and on the south side of the lantern of the central tower, to which he is also recorded as having given money. The money for the east window is not mentioned in Skirlaw's will, made in 1403 with later amendments, but there is no doubt of his donation, as his portrait, arms and dedicatory inscription appear in the window itself.

The nine-light east window is the biggest single expanse of stained glass in the Minster, visible in both Lady Chapel and choir. Its subject, unusual in stained glass,

64 Bishop Walter Skirlaw (1388–1406) of Durham, the donor of the east window, appears at its base. His arms decorate the altar frontal at which he kneels

OPPOSITE
65 The east window, glazed between 1405 and 1408 by the workshop of John Thornton of Coventry

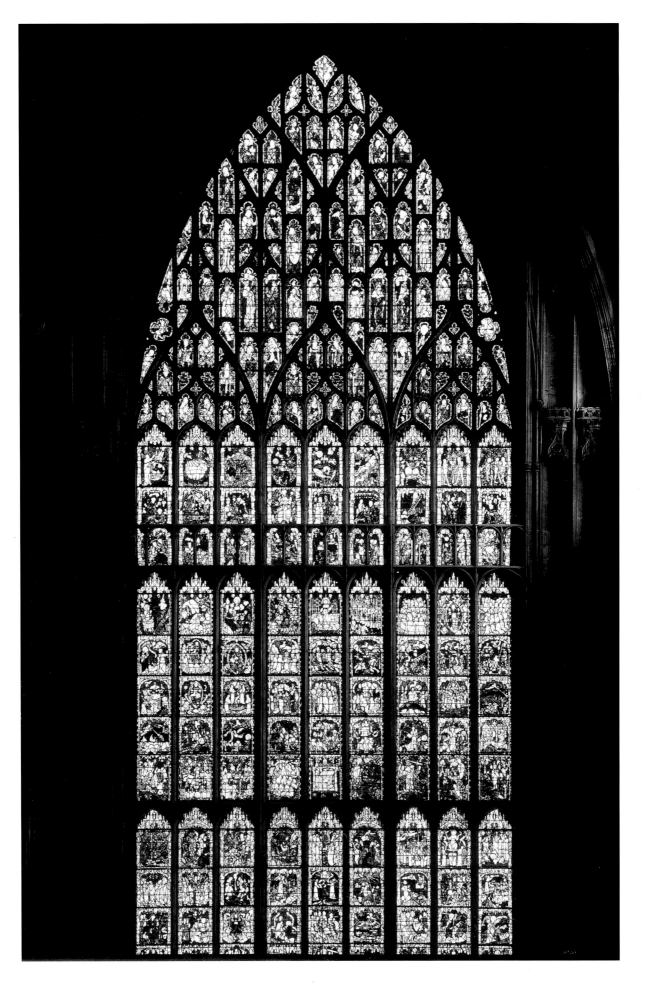

is appropriately ambitious, the history of the world from the beginning to the end, drawn from the first and last books of the Bible. The scene is set at the apex of the window in which a figure of Christ holds a book inscribed with the Latin words *Ego Sum Alpha et Omega* (I am the beginning and the end). The tracery is filled with 143 figures representing the heavenly hierarchy – Old Testament kings, prophets and patriarchs, the apostles, evangelists, saints, martyrs and the angelic orders. In the three rows of main light scenes above the gallery that runs across the window are 27 Old Testament scenes depicting the Creation to the death of Absalom. The following 81 scenes deal with events recorded in the Book of Revelation, while across the panels at the base of the window are enthroned figures representing the history of the church of York, together with the donor, Bishop Skirlaw.

The speed with which Thornton and his workshop were able to cartoon, paint and install this enormous commission suggests that he was given a model derived from an illuminated manuscript to work from. The content of the window would undoubtedly have been specified by Bishop Skirlaw, after discussion with the Chapter, the recipients of his gift, but it may also reflect ideas first contemplated by Archbishop Thoresby, for it is inconceivable that no thought had been given to the message to be conveyed in such a great wall of glass. A reliance upon a specific manuscript model is suggested by the division of the Revelation cycle into 81 scenes, 78 scenes of Apocalypse, with three prefatory scenes of the life of St John the Evangelist (67), conforming to a common Apocalypse cycle. The choice of historical figures for the base panels (70) was determined by the wooden tables of the Vicars Choral, the 'official' Minster history composed from various sources in the period 1388–97.

There is also reason to believe that there was a careful collaboration between patrons, glazier and mason in the design of the window tracery, inserted some time after the completion of the east wall, as its traceried top sits awkwardly on the capitals of the window jambs. The tracery admits 143 figures in main glazed openings, which as David O'Connor has recently pointed out, is remarkably close to the 144,000 witnesses described in the Book of Revelation.

66 Christ in Majesty at the apex of the east window, with the words *Ego sum A[lpha] et O[mega]* (I am the Beginning and the End), summarizing the entire message of the window

None of these observations on Thornton's sources can detract from his considerable imaginative and creative skill as a stained glass designer, for whatever the nature of his model, it was Thornton's job to translate this into a monumental window. The story has been 'edited' to suit the geometry of the window. The central light is used whenever possible to emphasize scenes or figures of particular importance and care was taken to ensure that related scenes were not split up between tiers of panels, especially at the end of a horizontal sequence. The figure of God the Father can easily be identified from a distance by the oval vesica that so often surrounds him. Certain scenes have been expanded for emphasis; God worshipped by the Elders (Rev. 4: 4–10), for example, has been spread across three panels, and God the Father is watched by St John who peers through a 'trap-door' in

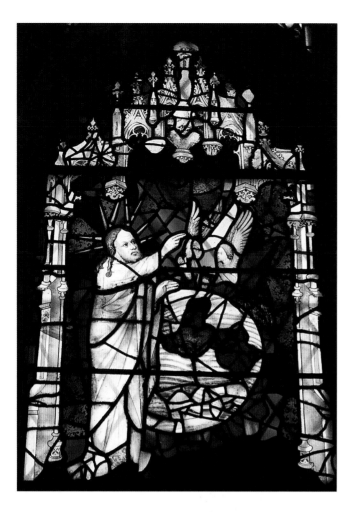

67 St John exiled to Patmos (east window). While modern scholarship has questioned the identification of the author of the Book of Revelation as the Evangelist, the east window follows the ancient tradition that they were one and the same

68 The first day of Creation – God the Father and the fall of the rebel angels (east window)

69 The temptation and fall of Adam and Eve (east window). The first man and woman are tempted to sin by a female-headed serpent

70 At the base of the east window, flanking the donor, are a series of historical figures including Kings William I, Edward the Confessor and Edward III

the bottom left of the panel. Thornton displays considerable ingenuity in translating the narrative into visual form. When St John is instructed to write to the seven churches (Rev. 1: 19), he and the angel look at an architectural structure filled with niches containing seven figures of archbishops. At 7: 1–2, the angels are described as standing at the corners of the world holding the winds. In the window (71) four angels at the corners of the panels hold robustly puffing, coarse-featured men's heads.

The window also reveals a careful reading of the biblical text. Scrolls of text report the spoken word. Narrative details are generally faithfully translated into visual detail. In the scene of the mighty angel and the seven thunders, for example, the angel is shown, as described in the text (Rev. 10: 1–7), with one foot on the sea and one on the land. In the emptying of the fifth vial (Rev. 16: 10), men are described as gnawing their tongues in pain, a detail effectively portrayed in Thornton's glass. In other instances, details are altered in order to make them more legible. In the panel of Christ and the seven candlesticks (73) (Rev. 1: 12–17), the text describes the son of man as having seven stars in his right hand. Thornton has enlarged the stars and placed them above Christ's right shoulder, where they can be seen more clearly.

RIGHT
71 The angels of the four winds (east window)

BELOW LEFT
72 John takes the book from the mighty angel (east window)

BELOW RIGHT
73 The Son of Man (east window)

The window is often criticized as being illegible from the ground. Poor repair and damage in the 1829 fire have certainly not improved legibility and heavy re-leading and the introduction of protective external glazing have further dulled the window. It is to be hoped that in any future conservation programme some of these issues can be addressed and the correct biblical order of all the panels be restored. These problems of visibility should not be over-emphasized, however. The heavenly Jerusalem was described as a structure of light and jewelled colour and the east window played a vital role in establishing the Minster's claim to be an earthly foretaste of the heavenly splendours to come.

The western choir

John Thornton remained in York after the completion of the east window. In 1410 he was made a freeman of the City, essential if he was to undertake commissions for patrons other than the Dean and Chapter. Glass in Thornton's style is to be found in a number of the City's parish churches, in addition to locations further afield in both the north-east and the Midlands. It is now appreciated that not all glass in the so-called 'York style' originated in York or in the workshop of John Thornton, although it is known that he retained property in Coventry and may even have continued to run a business there. Perhaps his greatest influence was felt in York, however, where he was still living in 1433, residing in property owned by the Dean and Chapter.

Only the east window is a documented work by John Thornton. Much work remains to be done on the style and workshop practices of Thornton and his associates, but the visual evidence supports the supposition that he and his workshop glazed the clerestory and aisles of the five bays of the western choir. Only the St Cuthbert window in the south choir transept (s7), glazed perhaps in the 1440s, may be the work of other glass-painters, and even then the debt to Thornton is clear.

The building of the western choir was the second stage in the redevelopment of the eastern arm. For some twenty years after Archbishop Thoresby's death the western bays of the twelfth-century choir continued in use. In 1394 the old choir was finally abandoned, and services transferred to the new vestries on the south side. The old choir was finally demolished, and the new choir rose up in an east-to-west programme, finally linking the Lady Chapel to the crossing. The exact sequence of construction remains to be determined, but by 1399 night watchmen were needed to safeguard what must have been an open building site. The first bay (74), encompassing the choir transepts, must have been completed at least to triforium level before 1405, because in the spandrels of the arcade are the arms of Archbishop Richard Scrope, elected in 1398 and executed by Henry IV in June 1405. His arms are accompanied by those of Bishop Walter Skirlaw (d.1406).

Progress was checked in 1407 by the collapse of the central tower. The extent of the damage is unclear, but the emergency was sufficiently serious to prompt the despatch to York of William Colchester, Henry IV's master mason. The work force was divided, with one team working on the choir and the other on the stabilization and reconstruction of the crossing. Heavy expenditure on building materials and the wages of the workforce show that work on the choir continued until at least 1415, a date supported by analysis of the heraldic evidence. The display of shields in the spandrels of the arcade, begun in the nave and continued into the Lady Chapel, was

extended into the choir. Heraldry also figures prominently in the lowest tier of panels in the clerestory windows.

The fire of 1829, which fed on the wood of the medieval choir stalls (which were totally destroyed) also did considerable damage to the stained glass, especially on the south side. None the less, eight windows in the clerestory (N8–N11 and S8–S11), three windows in the north aisle (n8–n10), one window in the south aisle (s9) and the windows of the choir transepts (n7 (the St William window), N6, N7, s7 (the St Cuthbert window), S6 and S7) survive.

The windows in the choir celebrate the triumph of Christianity in the north of England in general and the importance of the cathedral church of York in particular. The altar is lit by windows that portray the lives and miracles of St William (n7) and St Cuthbert (s7), but recessed in the choir transepts as they are, the windows would have been visible only to those celebrating mass. The most detailed exposition of the message is to be found in the clerestory windows, shining light onto the daily assembly of the Canons and the choir of the cathedral community seated in the stalls below – a luminous reminder of their historical and spiritual legacy. Despite the loss of many of the identifying labels, it is clear that the scheme represents those figures significant to the history of the church in the northern province from earliest times to the Anglo-Saxon conversion, with the majority of figures dating from the seventh and eighth centuries. This is the period described so vividly in Bede's *Ecclesiastical History of the English Nation*. Each window contains historical figures

74 The south side of the first bay of the western choir, decorated with the arms of Archbishop Richard Scrope (1398–1405) and the arms of Bishop Walter Skirlaw of Durham (1388–1406)

75 A King of England
(Henry IV?) and
St Paulinus in choir
clerestory N11

under canopies above a shield of arms commemorating a contemporary donor, many
of whom can be identified as members of the Chapter. The heraldry in the windows
supports a date of *c.*1408–*c.*1414 for this part of the glazing scheme. In each five-
light window the figures were arranged in the same way – bishop or archbishop,
king, pope, king, bishop or archbishop. Windows N11 and S11, nearest the crossing
tower, have only four lights. The figures are arranged chronologically, with the
earliest identifiable figures in window S11 – King Lucius of the Britons in the fourth
light, who according to Bede, wrote to Pope Eleutherius (*c.*174–89) who appears in
the third light, requesting help in converting Britain to Christianity. In window N11
(75) is the figure of a king holding a scroll with the words *Anglie et Francie* ([King]
of England and France), a title first claimed by King Edward III in 1340. The shield
beneath his feet is that of England in the form adopted by Henry IV in 1406 and
Dr Norton has pointed out that the features of the king bear a resemblance to those
of Henry on his tomb in Canterbury Cathedral.

   The care taken in the choice and arrangement of figures can be most easily
appreciated in the windows on the north side, which are best preserved. In window
N8 (76) St John of Beverley, Bishop of York (705–17) and his successor St Wilfrid II
(717–44) are accompanied by the saintly King Ceolwulf (729–37) and his successor
King Eadberht (737–48), brother of Archbishop Egberht of York, Wilfrid II's
successor. The pope is unidentified. The heraldry in the lower panels identifies the
donors as members of the Bowet family, relations of Archbishop Henry Bowet
(1407–23). In window N9 the two archbishops are St Wilfrid, Bishop of York in 669

(d.709), and St Bosa who succeeded him after his deposition. Pope Agatho, in the centre light, is the pope to whom Wilfrid appealed and who acquitted him of the charges made against him by Archbishop Theodore of Canterbury. The kings are Oswiu (655–70) who presided over the Synod of Whitby in 664 in which the cause of the Roman church triumphed over the customs of the Celtic tradition, and his son, King Aldfrith (685–705). The heraldry identifies the donor of the window – Henry, third Lord Scrope of Masham and nephew of Archbishop Scrope, and dates it to the period 1411–15. His arms appear in stone in the same bay.

The quality of the execution of the western choir clerestory windows is variable, far less consistently accomplished than either the east window or the St William window. It is clear, however, that the windows were designed as a single programme. They are not identical in detail. The canopy designs and the frames around the shields in the lower panels on the north and south sides are different, for example. There is, however, a noticeable reuse of cartoons on both sides of the choir, indicative of close workshop collaboration. The cartoon of the king in the second light of window N9, for example, is also used for the king in the second lights of N8 and N10, while the pope in the centre light of N8 is also used in the centre light of N9 and N10 and the fifth light of S8.

The choir transepts contain windows 75 feet in height, an expanse of glass

BELOW LEFT
76 Window N8, the gift of Archbishop Henry Bowet (1406–13) and his family. The figures, not all of them identifiable, have been made from the same cartoons as figures in N9

BELOW RIGHT
77 Window S10, containing the arms of Cardinal Beaufort, half-brother of Henry IV, and the arms of Minster Treasurer Thomas Haxey (1418–25). The canopies are of a different design from those on the north side

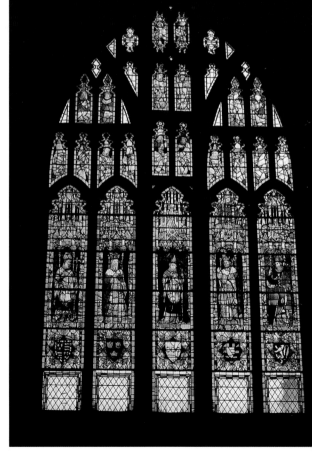

78 Beatrice de Ros
(d.1415), mother of
William, sixth Baron Ros,
and probably the donor
of the St William window,
c.1414 (n7)

rivalling the great windows at the east and west ends of the Cathedral. The cost of
filling these windows with stained glass was prodigious, beyond the resources of the
Dean and Chapter. As the glazing of the clerestory windows drew to a close, the
Dean and Chapter secured a donor for the window on the north side (n7). The honour
of paying for the most extensive pictorial cycle of the life, death and miracles of
St William, the Minster's 'resident' saint, whose shrine stood behind the high altar,
was claimed by the Ros family. The family of Ros of Helmsley had long been
associated with the Minster fabric. Their arms can be seen in the nave clerestory
windows, among the stone shields in the nave arcade, in the windows of the Lady
Chapel and in the Lady Chapel arcade. The Ros shield was also included in the
paintings added to the Chapter House vestibule c.1396, when Richard II came to
York to grant the city charter. Here the Ros lords are shown in company with the
King, Bishop Skirlaw and the Percys, also long-standing benefactors of the Minster.
The base panels of the St William window depict nine members of the Ros family,
dressed in heraldic surcoats and capes. The donor of the window is likely to have
been Beatrice (née Stafford), mother of William, the sixth baron (d.1414), who
outlived her son, dying in 1415.

Above the donor panels, enclosed in rectangular architectural frames, are 95
narrative panels recounting the story of St William from his birth to the miraculous
events that occurred at his original tomb in the nave and the shrine in the choir to
which his body was translated in 1284. St William's life was not one packed with the

sort of incident easily translated into a picture cycle. The most prominent events concern juridical disputes, in which the Archbishop was finally vindicated and reinstated to his See. Indeed, his triumphant return to York was the occasion of one of his most famous miracles (81), when he intervened to save those who had fallen into the river from the collapsed bridge over the Ouse.

The window depicts miraculous events associated with both St William's tomb (in the nave) and his shrine (in the choir), thus emphasizing the healing efficacy of a visit to the Minster. In several scenes pilgrims are shown offering wax models of those body parts for which a cure was sought and the shrine is shown surrounded by the models (82), similar to those actually found at Exeter Cathedral. The shrine that stood in the choir at the time that the window was made has since disappeared

82 The shrine of St William (n7). While the depiction of the shrine itself cannot be considered architecturally accurate, the practice of adorning shrines with models in wax or precious materials is well attested

without trace, replaced in 1472 by a larger structure, parts of which survive in the Yorkshire Museum. The shrine depicted in the window conforms to a standard shrine form, a base with gables and niches, and with an altar table at the west end. This image cannot be taken to be an accurate image of the shrine paid for by Bishop Bek, for the glass-painters have shown it as a perpendicular construction of the fifteenth century, rather than as a structure of 1284. In its size, which seems modest, the window is probably accurate. The new shrine was far larger, the largest shrine-base of the period.

The St William window is of such exceptional and consistently high quality that there can be little doubt that it is the work of John Thornton. Numerous comparisons with the east window tend to confirm this. It is to be hoped that the forthcoming conservation of the window will unravel more of its complexities and enable the individual hands of Thornton and his workshop to be much better appreciated. The equivalent window on the south side (s7) is of neither the same date nor the same quality. Having failed to find a donor for the window on the south side, the Dean and Chapter must have ordered it to be filled with temporary quarry glazing until a donor could be found.

The political uncertainties of the early years of the fifteenth century made a glazing scheme that celebrated the saintly ecclesiastics and kings of the distant past a very attractive choice to the York Chapter. In 1399, when work on the choir was well under way, Richard II, a benefactor of the Minster and granter of the city's charter, whose white hart emblem decorates the south-east crossing pier, was deposed and supplanted by his cousin Henry Bolingbroke. Archbishop Richard Scrope, whose brother Stephen, second Lord Scrope of Masham, had been a close associate of the deposed king, had accepted Richard II's renunciation of the throne and had sworn fealty to the new king, assisting at the coronation of Henry IV. In 1403 he celebrated high mass in the Minster in the King's presence. A window in the north aisle (n4), now lost, was probably donated by the King at this time. However, by 1405 the Archbishop had preached open rebellion against the Crown, resulting in his own execution and the temporary loss of the city's privileges. After his decapitation at Clementhorpe on 8 June 1405, the Archbishop escaped the fate of his co-conspirators, whose heads were placed on the city gates. Instead, his body was borne to the Minster for burial in St Stephen's Chapel, where it was soon the site of miracles and attracted large numbers of pilgrims. The King's officers discouraged this by erecting a barricade of logs and stones to keep the crowds at bay.

Although no churchman could condone the execution of an annointed archbishop by the secular authority, it is unlikely that the Dean and Chapter were especially sympathetic to their rebellious archbishop. Five vicars choral and a Minster chaplain had joined the rebellion and the Vicars Choral had carried his corpse back to the Minster. None the less, in the early years after his accession, the new king had striven to fill the church with as many of his own supporters as possible, and as a result the most important members of the Chapter were staunch Lancastrians, notably Dean Thomas Langley (1401–6) and Dean John Prophete (1406–16). Henry had first hoped to see Langley made Archbishop, but the Pope refused to co-operate, sending Langley to Durham instead. Henry then resisted all other papal provision and eventually secured the translation of Henry Bowet from Bath and Wells (84). Bowet was one of Henry's oldest and most loyal supporters and in 1413 the recently deceased king was remembered

in the chantry founded by Bowet in All Saints' Chapel. While Archbishop Scrope's family were benefactors to the fabric and their arms appear in a number of places in stone and glass, there is little evidence that they openly promoted his cult in the immediate aftermath of his death.

Support for the cult seems to have been strongest among the citizens of York, among whom Henry IV was unpopular. The rebels of 1405 had included many north Yorkshire knights from families that had traditionally supported the Minster fabric (including the Hastings, FitzRandolph and Colville families, who are all commemorated in the nave). That Henry's vengeance against the City was not more severe and long-lived owed much to the skilful diplomacy of the city government and the prompt payment of a large fine. None the less, tensions in the city must have run high in the aftermath of the rebellion.

The fall of the crossing tower in 1407 gave Henry an opportunity to display his generosity and placate public opinion in York. Master mason William Colchester was sent to take charge. Colchester and his servants were unpopular and suffered physical abuse at the hands of their fellow masons. While this action might have been an expression of professional jealousy, an antipathy to Colchester's royal master might also have been a factor. Whatever the explanation, it is clear that the glazing

83 The translation of St William's relics in 1284 (n7). This event, paid for by Bishop Bek of Durham, was attended by King Edward I, Queen Eleanor and many bishops and nobles

84 Archbishop Henry
Bowet (1407–23) in n10.
Although not King Henry's
first choice to succeed
Archbishop Scrope, he
had long been a supporter
of the new king

OPPOSITE ABOVE
85 The three saints chosen
by Canon Thomas Parker,
prebendary of Ampleforth
(1410–23) for n9 were
St John of Beverley,
St Thomas of Canterbury,
his name saint, and
St William of York

OPPOSITE BELOW
86 Treasurer Robert
Wolveden (1426–32),
donor of n8, chose as
subjects for his window
St Chad, first Bishop of
Lichfield, where Wolveden
was Precentor and
subsequently Dean,
St Paulinus, the first
bishop of York and
St Nicholas of Myra

of the choir was being planned and executed at a time of extraordinary tension and
sensitivity in the city, with the Chapter attempting to chart a course through a
potential minefield of devotional and political sensibilities.

The glazing of the choir aisle windows, at eye level and therefore especially
visible to those passing into or out of the choir, neatly avoided all controversy in the
choice of subject-matter. The design of the windows, which are best preserved on
the north side (n8–n10), was identical, and their stylistic homogeneity, linking them
to the St William window (n7) to the east, suggests that the windows were glazed in
a single campaign. Archbishop Bowet, who had already contributed to the clerestory
glazing, gave a lead, donating window n10. He was joined by Thomas Parker,
prebendary of Ampleforth (1410–23) and Treasurer Robert Wolveden (1426–32).
A date in the 1420s has been suggested for these windows, based on the date of
Wolveden's treasurership. He had a long career in the Minster hierarchy, however,
having become prebendary of Knaresborough in 1400, a position he exchanged for
that of prebendary of Wetwang in 1408, and on historical and stylistic grounds a
date of c.1415 seems more likely for these three windows.

Bowet chose St Peter, St Paul and the Virgin Mary for his window. St Peter and
St Paul are the two saints most commonly represented on the seals of the Archbishop, often, but not always accompanied by St William of York. Bowet's seal gives
pride of place to the Virgin Mary, who is flanked, as in the window, by St Peter and
St Paul. Thomas Parker, donor of window n9, was also rector of nearby Bolton Percy
and rebuilt and glazed the chancel there, a measure of his considerable wealth as a
residentiary canon of York. His window commemorates two of the Minster's sainted
bishops, John of Beverley and St William, and his own name saint, St Thomas of
Canterbury, including a unique depiction of Thomas as Chancellor (1155–62). Robert
Wolveden chose St Chad, St Paulinus and St Nicholas of Myra for his window (n8).

In the choice of Paulinus, first Bishop of York, and Chad, first Bishop of Lichfield, Wolveden was reflecting the dual aspects of his clerical career as Precentor of Lichfield from 1390, Canon of York from 1400 and both Treasurer of York and Dean of Lichfield from 1426.

In the final phases of the glazing of the choir, the influence of further changes in the political climate can be discerned. Window S6 was the gift of Stephen Scrope, Archdeacon of Richmond (1402–18), and contains a large image of Archbishop Richard Scrope, to whom a prayer is addressed, as if to a saint. The window is faced by a window of the same date given by Robert Wolveden, which depicts St William. A more tolerant climate prevailed during the reign of Henry V, who had interred the body of Richard II in Westminster Abbey, its intended resting place, and had finally fulfilled his father's penance for the death of Archbishop Scrope by founding three religious houses. The rehabilitation of Archbishop Scrope was now promoted by his family and was undoubtedly encouraged by the fact that his burial place in the Minster was proving to be a financial asset – the offerings at his grave in St Stephen's Chapel, which by the 1450s was known as Scrope's Chapel, considerably exceeded those at St William's shrine. In 1459 Thomas, fifth Lord Scrope of Masham established a chantry in St Stephen's chapel, already the place of burial of at least two other Scrope lords. The chapel was refurbished and it was likely at this time that the Archbishop was finally provided with a proper tomb chest.

The image of Archbishop Scrope, a victim of the Lancastrian monarchy, was eventually joined in the south choir transept by a window celebrating that dynasty. The main subject of window s7, the gift of Thomas Langley, Bishop of Durham and former Dean of York, is the life and miracles of St Cuthbert. A large figure of

87 Archbishop Richard Scrope (1398–1405) depicted in S6. The window was the gift of his kinsman Stephen Scrope, Archdeacon of Richmond (1402–18)

RIGHT
88 A Lancastrian 'Who's Who' fills the lower part of the St Cuthbert window (s7). The window was the gift of Thomas Langley, former Dean of York and from 1406 Bishop of Durham

St Cuthbert carrying the head of St Oswald is surrounded by Lancastrian kings and members of the Lancastrian episcopate (88). In the lower register are Archbishop Henry Bowet (d.1423), Cardinal Henry Beaufort, Bishop of Winchester (d.1447), Humphrey, Duke of Gloucester (d.1447), Cardinal John Kemp, Archbishop of York 1425–52 and Thomas Langley (d.1437) himself. Above the clerics are Henry V (d.1422), Henry VI (d.1471), John of Gaunt (d.1399) and Henry IV (d.1413). Bowet's loyalty to Henry IV had won him an archbishopric. Henry Beaufort was Henry IV's half-brother and he and Langley served as Chancellor to both Henry V and Henry VI. Kemp succeeded Beaufort as Chancellor to Henry VI. The window cannot have been commissioned earlier than 1426, when Beaufort was made Cardinal. Provision for the window is not mentioned in Langley's will of 1437, prompting J. T. Fowler to suggest that the window was erected during his lifetime. However, Kemp, who is described in the window as *Cardinalis Ebor*, was not made a cardinal until 1443. Henry VI is depicted in the windows as a crowned adult. Although his coronation took place in 1429, when he was a child of eight, he was not declared to be of age until 1437, supporting a date for the window in the early 1440s. In common with many windows on the south side of the cathedral, the St Cuthbert window has suffered damage. Indeed, J. T. Fowler even suggested that some panels had been deliberately defaced. Extensive repair was carried out by J. W. Knowles in 1887. Its legibility has certainly been diminished by the multitude of heavy mending leads. The quality of the glass-painting is variable and generally of a lower standard than the earlier St William window.

89 One of the better preserved scenes from the St Cuthbert window (s7), which like so many of the stories associated with the saint, involves the creatures and birds of the north

The triumph of the Yorkists under King Edward IV led to another shift in the fortunes of the Minster's imagery. Archbishop Scrope, executed by Henry IV, became something of a Yorkist hero. He is depicted as a saint in stained glass of *c*.1461–69 in the collegiate church of Fotheringhay, Northamptonshire, founded and endowed by the House of York. In 1462 the promotion of his canonization was seriously considered, but in the end came to nothing. If the triumph of the House of York improved the fortunes of the unofficial cult of Richard Scrope, it did little for that of the Lancastrian King Henry VI, also revered as a saint and commemorated on the stone choir screen. An image of Henry VI in the Minster had become an object of veneration and in 1479 Archbishop Lawrence Booth issued an admonition against any person expressing devotion to it. It is likely that the removal of the choir screen statue and the apparently deliberate defacement of the King's identity in the St Cuthbert window date from this time.

The End of the Middle Ages

By the early fifteenth century, the original thirteenth-century glazing of the transepts must have been showing signs of wear and tear. The widening of the choir at the end of the fourteenth century had resulted in the loss of a window in the two transept chapels on either side of the crossing, dedicated to St William (south side) and St Nicholas (north side). Further damage was no doubt sustained as a result of the fall of the central tower in 1407 and the reconstruction work that followed. By c.1425–30 this building work was drawing to a close and attention turned to reglazing the transept chapels.

Treasurer Robert Wolveden (1426–32), who had already contributed to the glazing of the choir, gave a lead. His name and coat of arms appear in both the chapels of St William and St Nicholas (sII and nII), suggesting that the reglazing programme began at the crossing and moved outwards. In 1434 the fabric rolls record payments for new stanchions for the windows of these chapels, which were described as newly glazed. This suggests that the windows were paid for posthumously, perhaps from the £20 bequeathed by Wolveden in his will. Other donors included Isabella and John Saxton, who kneel before St John the Baptist in window sI4. In the north transept the arms of Archbishop Scrope in window nI3 may reflect the patronage of John, fourth Lord Scrope of Masham (1418–55).

Despite the involvement of a number of different donors, the glazing of the transept chapels resulted in a coherent iconographic programme. Each one was provided with images in glass appropriate to the dedication of its altar. Those on the south side are best preserved and depict St William (sII), St Michael (sI2), the Archangel Gabriel (sI3), St John the Baptist (sI4) and the Virgin and Child (sI5). On the north side only the figures of St Nicholas of Myra (nII) and St Stephen (sI2) are fifteenth century. St George (sI6) and St Oswald (sI7) on the south side and St Lawrence (nI3), St Paul (nI4) and St Peter (nI5) on the north are all by the firm of C. E. Kempe & Co (1899–1902), although they replicate medieval figures recorded by Torr.

The figures in the transept chapels lack the refinement of those in the choir, although like so much fifteenth-century glass in York, they reveal the influence of John Thornton and his workshop. There are signs of financial restraint in their execution; cheaper white glass, enlivened with yellow stain, predominates. Figures are placed against simple quarries with a repeated star motif, rather than elaborate patterned and coloured backgrounds. Although they stand on projecting plinths with tiled pavements, there are no architectural canopies.

There are also signs of economy in the execution of the eight windows of the lantern tower (L/T NI–N4 and L/T

S1–4) in which 48 panels depicting variations of the crossed keys of St Peter are arranged in two registers, above and below the transoms. Each pair of keys is surrounded by a wreath of foliage with an entwined scroll. Coloured glass is used sparingly and the panels are rather coarsely executed. In 1471 a team of eight glaziers, led by Matthew Petty, was paid 1s per panel and the commission may have been rushed in order to be completed in time for the consecration of the Minster on 3 July 1472. It is interesting that one of the few glazing programmes to be funded entirely by the medieval Dean and Chapter was such a modest job. While economy may have determined the use of cheaper white glass, it was also important, of course, to ensure that the crossing was well lit by the lantern above, and colour was reserved for the painted vault for which pigments were bought in 1472.

The original glazing of the south transept rose and the windows of the south wall survived into the early sixteenth century. The rose window was then reglazed with glass decorated with stems bearing double roses representing the union of the warring houses of York and Lancaster, effected by the marriage of Henry VII and Elizabeth of York in 1486. It is unlikely that the window is quite as early as this, although the window is apparently an allusion to the marriage that helped to stabilize the Tudor monarchy. A fragment of the arms of Archbishop Thomas Savage (1501–7) survives in s22 and it was during his archiepiscopate that the further embellishment of the south transept was taking place. In 1507 the executors of Archdeacon John Reynald (d.1506) erected new wooden screens in the east aisle of the south transept. Until the eighteenth century, window s23 contained an image of the Virgin and Child and a memorial panel to glazier and Lord Mayor John Petty (d.1508). The date of his death was recorded under his figure kneeling at a prie-dieu, accompanied by the arms of the Glaziers' Company. It is possible that John Petty, son of Matthew, was responsible for the rose window and for the figures of St William, St Peter, St Paul and St Wilfrid (93) that survive in the windows above the south door (s20–s22).

In a paper devoted to sixteenth-century glass in the Minster, published in 1960, Dean Milner-White pointed out similarities between the York glass and windows of *c.*1500–15 in Fairford parish church in Gloucestershire. The Fairford windows are likely to be the work of Anglo-Netherlandish glass-painters, who settled in the Southwark area of London in increasing numbers in the last quarter of the fifteenth century. In 1497 one of their number, Barnard Flower, was made King's Glazier and supplied glass for such prestigious royal commissions as Richmond Palace and the new Lady Chapel at Westminster Abbey. The York windows share many

92 The early sixteenth-century rose window (S16). The white and red Tudor roses recall the union of the warring houses of York and Lancaster in the persons of Henry VII and his queen Elizabeth of York

of the painterly characteristics of the Fairford windows and the treatment of architectural niches, pierced by round-headed windows and lined with richly brocaded fabrics, is alike in each. The Minster glass is not of comparable quality, however, and its impact has been further diminished by damage and inelegant repair.

It is fitting that the history of the medieval Minster's *in situ* glazing, which began in the south transept, should also finish there. While it could be argued that by the sixteenth century the most innovative work in English stained glass emanated from London rather than York, it is none the less apparent that the York glaziers continued to be responsive to artistic developments within their craft. The vigour of the York craft on the very eve of the Reformation that was to herald its decline can be judged from a series of panels of *c.*1535 depicting the early life of St Thomas Becket. Nine panels from this series, unfairly dismissed by J. A. Knowles as 'coarse in character and brutal in execution', are now located in the east window of the Chapter House. A further four panels are in nearby St Michael le Belfrey. The glass-painting has a monumental quality and a narrative vigour demonstrating that the glass-painters of sixteenth-century York still had plenty to offer.

ABOVE LEFT
93 St Peter and St Paul in s21, was glazed in the first quarter of the sixteenth century and repaired in the 1780s by William Peckitt

ABOVE RIGHT
94 The infant St Thomas Becket brought to be educated (Chapter House east window, *c.*1535). The Becket panels were not made for the Minster and may have originated in St Wilfrid's parish church

After the Reformation

By the early sixteenth century almost every window in the Minster had been filled with medieval glass, leaving very few opportunities for glass-painters of successive generations. Furthermore, the religious changes of the Reformation severely reduced the demand for religious stained glass and in some parts of England resulted in its removal and destruction. There is little evidence of serious iconoclasm directed against the Minster's windows, although the city's monastic and friary churches were not spared. The major casualties in the Minster were the objects associated with the cult of St William. In October 1541 the silver-gilt head shrine was broken up and both the marble shrine base in the choir and the tomb in the nave were dismantled. In the reign of the overtly Protestant Edward VI images in stained glass were proscribed in injunctions against superstitious imagery for the first time, but in the Minster it was the plate and the vestments associated with the old religion that were swept away.

Some damage to stained glass was sustained during the siege of York in the summer of 1644. The royalist congregations in the nave were disturbed by the noise of the Parliamentarian siege guns and by the occasional bullet that came through a window and bounced from pillar to pillar. The city surrendered in the middle of July, and the historic fabric of the city and the Minster were preserved thanks to the intervention of the Parliamentary commander, Thomas, Lord Fairfax, a Yorkshireman and a lover of antiquities. The Minster did not escape entirely unscathed, although it was not subjected to the vandalism suffered by Lichfield, Peterborough or Durham cathedrals. Many of its brasses were lost, pulled up for their scrap value, and some damage to glass and sculpture in the Chapter House may be attributable to this period. Torr described the westernmost windows of the nave aisles as having been removed 'during the late troubles'. However, over £1,000 was said to have been spent on the Minster fabric during the Interregnum – Torr recorded the date 1658 in one of the Chapter House windows – and the overall impression conveyed by the late seventeenth-century antiquaries is of a Minster filled with medieval glass.

In the years after the restoration of the Monarchy in 1660, repairs were made to damaged roofs and windows. Sir John Petty's memorial window in s23 had been restored in 1662 by Edmund Gyles (1611–76). In the 1690s further repairs to the Chapter House windows were undertaken by a glazier called Charles Crosby. Edmund Gyles's son, Henry (1645–1709), was also paid for repairs to the Minster's windows and this work may have included the east window. Very little new glass was commissioned, however. An armorial of Archbishop Lamplugh (96) in s6 was made by Gyles in 1691, the only substantial surviving relic in the Minster of the work of this largely self-taught York glass-painter, the most important stained glass artist of his generation. The technique employed is very different from that seen in the medieval windows. Transparent coloured enamels were applied and fired onto white glass, largely eliminating the need for pot-metal coloured glass. In the case of the Lamplugh shield, much of the coloured enamel has flaked away, leaving only yellow stain.

By the middle of the eighteenth century the most prominent practitioner of enamel glass-painting was William Peckitt of York (1731–95), like Henry Gyles, self-taught and a life-long experimenter in the techniques of his craft. Throughout his career Peckitt enjoyed the patronage of Dean Fountayne (1747–1802) and as a result was employed both to repair ancient glass and to supply new windows for the Minster. Evidence of his restoration work can still be seen in the tracery lights of a number of nave windows. Good-quality pot-metal glasses suitable for stained glass were in short supply and the dates in coloured glass in the nave (for example, 1789 in s33, 1779 in n27) are in rather garish colours, probably supplied by Peckitt, although installed by the Minster's own glaziers. In 1757 Peckitt supplied new painted glass to make good deficiencies in the west window, including new heads, notably for the bishops and archbishops. In the following year figures of St John the Evangelist and St Peter were installed in the place of donor figures in the base of n30 and s36. The lower half of Eve and the serpent was inserted in nave window s30 in 1782. In 1765 Peckitt had painted a new west window for the chapel of New College, Oxford, accepting the displaced medieval glass in part payment (62). The exact date of its insertion in York Minster is not known, but it was probably installed in s8 in the 1780s.

Peckitt's most significant work in the Minster is the series of figures in the south transept (s18 and s19, s23 and s24). The earliest figure, that of St Peter, was installed in 1754, but proved to be technically deficient, and in 1768 the badly flaking figure was replaced free of charge. The new St Peter (95) was made from a cartoon by Sir James Thornhill, first used in 1766 in the west window of Exeter Cathedral. In 1780 Peckitt painted two further figures, of Abraham and Solomon. The figure of Moses, which completes the quartet, cannot be dated with certainty, but like the figure of Abraham, was taken from a design of 1774 originally prepared for New College chapel by Biagio Rebecca. Peckitt's draughtsmanship was his weakness and his best work is therefore that based on cartoons prepared by more proficient designers. Although in 1791 and 1793 Peckitt supplied new painted repairs for the windows of both transepts, including the Five Sisters and rose window, the figures of Abraham, Solomon and Moses were not installed during his lifetime. It is a mark of the Dean and Chapter's esteem for the 'late ingenious Mr William Peckitt' that after his death the Minster acquired the three figures from his widow. The windows illustrate the importance of the handling of ancient glass to the development of the skills of eighteenth-century glass painters. An echo of New College is found not only in the reuse of cartoons, but also in the interesting adaptation of New College's medieval canopy designs for use in an eighteenth-century version of a gothic architectural setting.

96 The arms of Archbishop
Lamplugh (1688–91), made
in 1691 by Henry Gyles (s6)

The Nineteenth and Twentieth Centuries

Although York Minster was studied and admired by stained glass artists of the nineteenth-century Gothic Revival, it offered them few opportunities to display their talents. Although many windows of exceptional quality were produced in the nineteenth century, the Minster can boast no great window by one of the masters of the period. A series of memorial windows by the firm of Clayton & Bell was installed in the KOYLI (King's Own Yorkshire Light Infantry) chapel (windows n19–n22) in 1862, but was removed in 1945 to make way for the medieval glass from St John's, Micklegate. The windows of 1899–1902 by the firm of C. E. Kempe & Co. in the windows opposite have already been mentioned. Their style is broadly sympathetic to the fifteenth-century figures they complement, although the figures of Saints Lawrence, Paul, Peter, George (99) and Oswald are rather more richly dressed than their medieval companions.

For the most part, the contribution of the nineteenth century has been in the restoration of the Minster's medieval heritage and this history cannot be fully explored here. Following the nave fire of 1840 the Newcastle glass-painter William Wailes was employed at the expense of his more eminent contemporary, Thomas Willement, the preferred choice of Minster architect Sydney Smirke. Wailes's work was confined to patching and the replacement of some of the damaged shields in the clerestory. His work as a restorer is perhaps better judged in All Saints, North Street. During the 1844–5 restoration of the Chapter House under Smirke's direction, the windows were entrusted to the York firm of John Barnett & Son. Barnett made careful tracings of the medieval glass, replacing those fragments that the simple restoration techniques of the day could not save. In the case of the east window this meant returning a facsimile rather than a medieval window (98). This sort of drastic restoration was only just beginning to be perceived as inappropriate and Barnett's efforts were favourably received by his contemporaries. The Barnett panels were removed from the Chapter House in 1959 and their subject-matter, and the skill with which they were copied from the lost thirteenth-century originals, are difficult to appreciate in their new location in the nave clerestory (N19, N20, S21 and S22).

A more cautious approach was adopted for the restoration of the St Cuthbert window in 1887 and the St William window in 1895, both restored by the York craftsman and glass historian J. W. Knowles, father of J. A. Knowles, author of one of the most important works on York's medieval stained glass. Some new glass was introduced into the windows, but not at the expense of the medieval glass, and the reordering was undertaken according to scholarly advice and only after careful examination of the panels. This collaboration of craftsmanship and scholarship is the basis on which modern conservation programmes proceed. It is all the more surprising, therefore, that in 1903 the restoration of the Mauley window in the nave (s32) by the London firm of Burlison & Grylls resulted in the loss of a medieval window and its replacement by a near-facsimile. It is none the less a superb copy of what pre-restoration photographs show to have been a heavily corroded window.

OPPOSITE
97 Ervin Bossanyi began his artistic career in his native Hungary. The rise of Fascism and anti-Semitism in his home-land took him to Germany, where he first worked in stained glass. The rise of the Nazis led to his departure to England. These panels, made in 1944, exemplify both his distinctive style and his consummate craftsmanship

OPPOSITE

98 An 1844 copy by John Barnett of the late thirteenth-century entombment of Christ from the Chapter House east window. The panel is now located in the nave clerestory (S22)

RIGHT

99 St George (s16) by the studio of C. E. Kempe & Co, which undertook restoration in the Minster between 1899 and 1903

The Minster's windows were removed for safety during both World Wars and in the years after 1945 the Minster glaziers undertook an extensive programme of restoration, much of it directed and chronicled by Dean Eric Milner-White (1941–63). Aspects of this programme were far more interventionist than would be deemed justifiable by today's conservators, but the Dean's enthusiasm and encouragement did much to establish York as a centre for the study and conservation of stained glass. He was also responsible for the acquisition by the Minster of historic glass from other locations – the Minster boasts an interesting collection of sixteenth and seventeenth-century windows, alienated from Rouen churches (see n3, s3 and s6). The contributions of modern stained glass artists have been limited to a small number of armorial and decorative panels (by Harry Stammers in window s10, for example). The most notable modern glass is located in the Zouche Chapel – the two panels depicting St Francis made in 1944 (97) by Hungarian emigré artist Ervin Bossanyi (1891–1975).

The history of the restoration of medieval stained glass in York culminated in the establishment in 1967 of the York Glaziers' Trust (100), one of a small number of specialist stained glass conservation studios. The growth of stained glass studies in the Centre for Medieval Studies of the University of York has ensured that craftsmanship has been matched by scholarship. With the Trust firmly established as a centre of excellence, the future of the Minster's stained glass is assured.

100 The conservators of the York Glaziers' Trust at work

Further Reading

Alexander, J. and Binski, P. *The Age of Chivalry. Art in Plantagenet England 1200–1400*, London 1987

Aylmer, G. E. and Cant, R. (eds). *A History of York Minster*, Oxford 1979

Benson, George. *The Ancient Painted Glass Windows in the Minster and Churches of the City of York*, Annual Report of the Yorkshire Philosophical Society, 1915

Brighton, Trevor. 'Henry Gyles. Virtuoso and Glasspainter of York, 1645–1709', *York Historian 4*, 1984

Brighton, Trevor and Sprakes, Brian. 'Medieval and Georgian Stained Glass in Oxford and Yorkshire. The work of Thomas of Oxford (1382–1427) and William Peckitt of York (1731–95) in New College Chapel, York Minster and St James, High Melton', *The Antiquaries Journal LXX* Part II, 1990, pp.380–415

Brown, Sarah and O'Connor, David. *Medieval Craftsmen: Glass-Painters*, London 1991

Browne, John. *The History of the Metropolitan Church of St Peter, York*, 2 vols, London 1847

Caviness, Madeline. 'Stained Glass' in *English Romanesque Art 1066–1200*, Exhibition Catalogue, Hayward Gallery, London 1984

Coldstream, Nicola. 'York Chapter House', *Journal of the British Archaeological Association CXXV*, 1972, pp.15–23

Drake, Francis. *Eboracum, or The History and Antiquities of the City of York*, London 1736

Fowler, James. 'On a window representing the Life and Miracles of St William of York at the north end of the eastern transept, York Minster', *Yorkshire Archaeological Journal 3*, 1873–74, pp.198–343

Fowler, J. T. 'On the St Cuthbert window in York Minster', *Yorkshire Archaeological Journal 4*, 1875–6, pp.249–376

French, T. W. 'Observations on some medieval glass in York Minster', *The Antiquaries Journal LI*, 1971, pp.86–93

———. 'The Dating of the Lady Chapel in York Minster', *The Antiquaries Journal LIV*, 1972, pp.309–19

———. 'The West Windows of York Minster', *The Yorkshire Archaeological Journal 47*, 1975, pp.81–5

———. 'The glazing of the St William window in York Minster', *Journal of the British Archaeological Association CXL*, 1987, pp.175–81

———. 'The Dating of York Minster Choir', *The Yorkshire Archaeological Journal 64*, 1992, pp.123–33

———. 'The glazing of the Lady Chapel Clerestory', *Friends of York Minster Annual Report 66*, 1995, pp.40–51

———. *York Minster. The Great East Window*. Corpus Vitrearum Medii Aevi, Great Britain, Summary Catalogue 2, London 1995

——— and O'Connor, David. *York Minster. A Catalogue of Medieval Stained Glass. Fascicule 1 The West Windows of the Nave*, Corpus Vitrearum Medii Aevi, Great Britain, III, London 1987

Harrison, F. *The Painted Glass of York*, London 1927

———. 'The West Choir Clerestory Windows in York Minster', *Yorkshire Archaeological Journal 26* 1922, pp.353–73

Knowles, J. A. *Essays in the History of the York School of Glass-Painting*, London 1936

Marks, Richard. *Stained Glass in England during the Middle Ages*, London 1993

Milner-White, E. *Sixteenth-Century Glass in York Minster and in the Church of St Michael le Belfrey*, St Antony's Hall Publications 17, York 1960

Norton, Christopher. 'The Medieval Paintings in the Chapter House', *Friends of York Minster Annual* Report 67, 1996, pp.34–51

———. 'Klosterneuburg and York: Artistic Cross-Currents at an English Cathedral c.1330', *Wiener Jahrbuch für Kunstgeschichte*, XLVI/XLVII, 1993/4, pp.519–32

———. 'Richard II and York Minster', in Rees Jones, Sarah (ed.) *The Government of Medieval York. Essays in Commemoration of the 1396 Royal Charter*, Borthwick Studies in History 3, York, 1997, pp.56–87

O'Connor, David and Haselock, Jeremy. 'The Stained and Painted Glass', in Aylmer and Cant (eds.),1979, pp. 313–93

[Bede] Sherley-Price, L. and Latham, R. E. (ed. & trans.) *A History of the English Church and People*, Harmondsworth 1976

Toy, John. *A Guide and Index to the Windows of York Minster*, York 1985

Webb, J. F. and Farmer, D. H. (ed. & trans.). *The Age of Bede*, Harmondsworth 1985

Willey, Ann. *York Minster*, London 1998

Wilson, Christopher. *The Gothic Cathedral and the Architecture of the Great Church 1130–1530*, London 1990

Winston, Charles. 'On the Painted Glass in the Cathedral and Churches of York' and Walford, W. S. 'On an heraldic Window in the North Aisle of the Nave of York Cathedral', in *Memoirs Illustrative of the Art of Glass-Painting*, London 1865

Index

Figures in **bold** refer to the illustrations